Human Connection

From an Open Adoption Journey

By

PAULA KANANI WEEKS

Contents

Introduction

I am an artist. As a young girl I started with pencils, then moved to paint and brushes, finally landing on film, negatives, 35mm lenses, and digital photography. Later, as a mother to young children, I mostly played with crayons, Play-doh, and Elmer's glue. I have contemplated many times how my gifts in art relate to the human connection.

I have learned a person's story begins clean and fresh, just as a work of art begins as a blank piece of paper or canvas. God is the ultimate Artist. Our stories are molded through lessons learned in life, a collaboration between His plan and our efforts to grow.

The canvas is blank. It waits, anticipating how the Artist will craft it into a masterpiece. It longs to be a thought-provoking story, a composed work of art, a crafted tapestry, an elegant score. But the Artist has His own plan for His canvas, it will indeed become a masterpiece, though maybe not in the way the canvas expected

The heart and soul of the final piece always comes from the thought behind brushstroke, the scuffle behind the pen. It is the journey along the way that creates the true story of our lives. The beauty of any journey is what we learn and allow the soul of the artwork to mold us into as we go.

This book grew from the living and breathing journey my husband and I have experienced through our beautiful adventures in open adoption. I say it is living and breathing because we work at our relationships within our open adoption community every day. The life lessons and values we have obtained are priceless, yet very much within reach. The most important lesson we have learned through our experience is the importance of human connections.

One of the keystones of meaningful human connection is communication. Not just a casual conversation in the street, though those also have value, but the kind of deep communication where we are willing to be vulnerable. Where we walk away changed—in our souls, in our hearts, and even in our outlook toward the community around us.

I have learned that human connection can grow from good communication, or crack under the pressure of broken communication. One evening, when my first two children were beyond the toddler years and entering childhood, my phone chimed, distracting me from a book I was reading to my children. I pulled it out of my pocket to view the message. Small black letters stared at me from the bright screen: "Do you still want a baby?" My heart raced and I swallowed hard against an obnoxious lump in the back of my throat. It began to swell as tears worked their way up into my eyes. A few tears appeared as I stared at the text. My children looked up at me, "Mom, are you ok?"

I was a little stunned. I honestly thought someone was playing a joke on me. "What a silly question to ask," I thought. "I always want more children." I typed my reply, "Yes, of course we do."

We proceeded to pursue the relationship. The birth mom and I texted and talked through Facetime several times a day, every day. She was having twins! We could be changing from a family of four to a family of six. I was excited, but also getting very concerned because the birth mom didn't seem to want to confirm her pregnancy with an agency, or even work with one.

The more we got to know her, the quicker we realized she was simply seeking love and attention without the intention to place a baby for adoption. In fact, there was no baby. Sadly, when we realized the truth, she disappeared. I was baffled and heartbroken. Having been built on false pretenses, the relationship crumbled. The reality of an authentic human connection with this young girl quickly disappeared without a solid foundation of honest communication.

Conversely, we have built a strong connection with our children's birth families through open and honest communication. I regularly have the opportunity to share intimate and daily details with my children's first families that build our connection with them and let them know they are never forgotten in our home. For example, whenever my son laughs, it reminds me of his birth mom—it is the exact same laugh. We are able to share his beautiful qualities and the connection he has to her. These are some of the blessings that open adoption can offer. A real connection not only through biology, but the open lines of communication we have in our open adoptions create strong emotional, or what I like to call, human connections. In an open adoption you are developing relationships with initially perfect strangers. The ability to allow for such relationships comes from our ability to offer an authentic human connection and the willingness to accept the same in return.

When tears filled her eyes and she shared with us her deep emotions about how she wasn't sure how to handle open adoption, this is a moment when I felt an authentic connection to her. Jerica, our oldest daughter's birth mom was graduating high school, her friends were leaving for college, life was about to change for her, and then she heard Kya say the word, "mama". Kya spoke those words to me, while we were visiting Jerica for the weekend. This tipped the emotional roller coaster straight down the rails for her. In that moment, she questioned open adoption. What was so empowering was the conversation that followed and truly built an honest connection between us all. She spoke her truth; she embraced the reality that this could change the course of our relationship and she allowed the emotions to naturally run their course. Because of the openness we already shared, this is when I learned a great deal of how human connections are obtained. Ultimately, she chose to stay open. She wanted to know Kya and watch her grow. Which of course we were elated about, that was our choice as well. We loved her and didn't want to lose her from our daily lives either. This real connection set the tone for the rest of the story, our open adoption story.

I use the acronym O.P.E.N. to discuss human connection in this book, and expand each letter into the following related words that encompass many of the nuggets of knowledge I've gained:

O: Obtainability, Optimism

P: Persevere, Perspective, Patience

E: Embrace, Empathy, Encompass

N: Nourish, Natural

Each of these qualities make up the lifeblood of both successful open adoptions and successful human connections in general. They lead to an open heart and mind and resilience to life's struggles.

Our experience with open adoption led us to a deeper understanding of our need for human connection, and a better understanding of how to achieve that connection. It is my hope that sharing the lessons we learned through our journey will help you along your own—whatever it may look like.

☙ CHAPTER 1 ❧

"O"pen

**"Optimism is the faith that leads to achievement.
Nothing can be done without hope and confidence."
-Helen Keller**

If I may be so bold to add to what Helen Keller is trying to teach, that it takes optimism and faith to be able to obtain the achievement you are looking for. If you want to obtain a valuable human connection with someone, you must be willing to have an optimistic view of not only those whom you wish to connect with but the outcome you are seeking.

Obtainability

"God often uses our deepest pain as the launching pad of our greatest calling." -unknown

My greatest desire was to become a mother. My deepest pain has been our infertility journey. My greatest calling has been to be a mother to the three amazing children God placed in our hearts and home through adoption.

During the moments of pain with the sting of infertility; my head in my hands, my face burning with tears streaming down my cheeks, I sought for the comfort. I had the distinct impression that the Savior was sitting next to me, carrying me. Those moments gave me assurance that God was composing His calling He had for my life. In His time, three of those callings came and are now my greatest blessings. With faith in His plan, righteous desires become obtainable and within arm's reach.

"A nose is a nose like a rose is a rose, as everybody knows, but may we propose that the rosiest nose is a one that plainly shows. . . ." Laughter filled the room as my siblings and I watched a new movie. The scene: a local TV station wanted to showcase a family with seven children. Friends of one of the boys made fun of the large number of children. How absurd! Seven kids? Who would even dare? Well, I was in a family of seven kids and it was grand. I thought, "Who wouldn't want a large family? The more the merrier, right?"

In a different scene in the movie, near the beginning, all the kids are in heaven, talking about what their fears are for Earth life. The oldest sister says, "My number one fear is that I will have nothing but a sweet spirit, but, with beauty or without, as long as I can dance my way through life, well, that's all that matters."

As the movie continues, all seven kids are on Earth together as a family. Big sister is in a wheelchair. Born with a birth defect, her beautiful dancing legs rested unmoving in a chair. As a young 12-year-old girl, this affected me. I remember vividly feeling so bad for her. Why would the one thing she wanted most be her trial on earth? How was she dealing with that?

I thought to myself, what is the one thing I want the most in this life? What is the one thing I would give anything to have or to be? Motherhood. Yes, being a mother, that was what my young mind thought of as the most important thing to me. The thought crept in like a mother to her sleeping child, "*That will be my trial. The ability to be a mother will be my greatest challenge.*" The thought shook me to my core, and yet, as a young teenage girl I didn't really think twice about it. Poof, just like that the thought and the heavy feeling that came with it disappeared from my mind for many years. After all, I didn't need to be worrying about that. I was just trying to get through zits, and puberty, and dealing with the fact that I was taller than all the boys.

What would you do if the one thing you wanted was unobtainable, or would end up being your greatest challenge?

Stop and take a minute to think about what it is that you wish to have in life. It's not bad to desire things. However, your intentions and the way you go about obtaining those things is important to consider. We obtain our blessings after we gain knowledge and experience in life's lessons. In the King James Version of the Bible, in John, chapter five, Jesus heals a man on a Sunday and then is judged by men for doing so. He then testifies that He is the Son of God. The Jews did not believe. In verse 39, he said this, "Search the scriptures; for in them ye think ye have eternal life: and they are they which testify of me." To fully obtain God's blessings and understand His plan for us, we must first seek to know Him and gain the knowledge of His truth.

The Book of Mormon, Another Testament of Jesus Christ, also talks about how He is a God of truth. In Ether, chapter three, God shows his finger to the brother of Jared as he touches sixteen stones to create light in the Jaredite boats on their long journey. In verse twelve, it reads, "Yea Lord, I know that thou speakest truth, for thou art a God of truth, and canst not lie." Obtainability of God's blessings come only after we obtain the truth and know God.

Thirty years after that 12-year-old girl was given a sneak peek into what her life would be, it has been proven to me that I am not the orchestrator of my life. When I was young, I had my life planned out to a "T." I knew I was going to marry, how many children we would have, and even their names. I knew what kind of mother I wanted to be. I knew that it didn't matter where I lived, as long as I had a crew of little ones following behind me like a mother duck and her ducklings crossing the road. It didn't matter how busy the road was because I had all my children following me on this journey and we were being watched over by our maker, God himself.

I learned in time that my Father in Heaven had a different path for me. I had big dreams of traveling the world as a fashion designer/photographer, of course while maintaining the desire to be a mother. I was so naïve to the reality of what being a career woman/mother looked like. Let alone wanting to travel while doing so. I began this dream by studying photography in college. Black and white film photography was my medium. Digital photography didn't come until a few years later. Did I just date myself?

Then, while working as a nanny in San Diego, I was inspired by a book by Richard Paul Evans that featured a young girl who visits an older woman and listens to her life story. After returning home from my year as a nanny, I found a job at a nursing home. Due to my experience caring for the elderly, I decided to go to nursing school. Though I went from big city traveler and fashion photographer to a nursing student in a small town, I loved the path that God placed in front of me. I loved working with those in need, and I loved the idea of being able to serve others through the healthcare system. I loved the stories the residents told and the connections I was creating with them. God was giving me opportunities I had never thought of for myself. He was allowing me to see all the great things I could do in my life for others in medicine, in health, and through exploring human connections in this arena. I was beginning to see how obtainable happiness was and how happiness plays an essential role in the development of human connections. My faith was developing as I learned to rely on Him. Only through Him and His plans for me was all this obtainable.

Having dreams and goals and plans gives us our agency to choose, our freedom to make decisions for ourselves, and even some focus of things to work on or work for. One of the greatest gifts we have been given is our free agency. However, we can easily find ourselves lost in our own agenda. This isn't wrong unless it keeps you from making important human connections. However, if God has a greater journey for us, He will gently guide us to refocus. With the same respect, He will allow us to see how His plans are obtainable and, through faith in Him, within reach.

Let's talk about obtaining genuine human connections for a moment. This is an action we choose and must actively participate in. Cheyenne Diaz, a writer for the Mindvalley blog, shared several ways in which human connections are made in an article from February 2019. Here are a few of the thoughts she collected from world-renowned speaker Sean Stephenson, the Dalai Lama, several presidents of the United States, and billionaire Richard Branson.

1)   "Be with people in the moment and learn their name."

We can physically be with someone, and still not share the moment with them. Often, we are so focused on our own moments that we neglect to acknowledge their moments. Stop to learn people's names and respect the moments they are living in.

During my experience with infertility, I found myself becoming more and more disconnected with people, especially in groups of women who were talking about pregnancy, birth stories, or related topics. I had gone from being a social butterfly as a kid, to an "everybody is my friend" teen, to a "how can I connect" adult. I felt like I had nothing to offer in these situations. However, connecting with other humans is not always about your story and what you must share. Yes, we all have something to offer in conversations and everyone has a story to tell. But we are often more concerned with telling our story than listening to another's. I know this to be true, as I have struggled to come back into a world of authentic human connections from my own little piece of the universe. I have found that we lose that human connection we all need when our focus is constantly inward. Instead, we need to seek for the emotions they are sharing and really wrap our arms around what they are giving.

We live in a world where we can see what a neighbor did yesterday at the click of a button. But how much more meaningful and connected would we be if instead we walked across the street and talked with that neighbor face-to-face, making eye contact, about her experiences. You get the idea. Learn people's names, hear their stories, and be in their moments with them.

2)   "Physical touch."

This is an obvious human connection as you are literally connected in touch, appropriate physical touch is what I'm talking about. Unfortunately, this is a tough human connection to obtain in today's world. I am usually a hugger, but with the fear of spreading disease during this COVID-19 pandemic, I've adopted what I like to call "air hugs." It's pretty self-explanatory. You open your arms wide and slightly lean in without actually touching. It breaks my heart to not be able to feel the warmth of another's touch, to have a strong embrace where you can hear their breath and or feel their heartbeat.

I don't know when casual physical touch will happen again, and honestly, we've lost a lot of our physical touch by virtue of living in a technology-driven world. We've gotten so accustomed to social media and using technology that we are losing the ability to find authentic human connections through something as simple as a handshake. However, I hope and pray that hugs and handshakes are back into play by the time this book is published.

3)   "Compassion for others."

The Dalai Lama says that compassion and always thinking of others is the true way to happiness. In my faith we call this ministering to others. The Dalai Lama also taught, "when you see someone don't look for what is wrong with them, look for what is right with them." Having compassion and looking for the good in others, then ministering to that person, whether virtually or personally, helps a human connection to be made.

Early on in our adoption journey, when we were contacted by a birth mom, we met with her in person shortly after our first email conversation. We sat with her, across a small café table eating ice cream. Sharing with each other our stories, she reached across the table and grabbed my hand. Those precious words came out of her mouth, "I want you to be the parents of my child". I felt love for her in that moment, I had compassion for her story and for her unborn child. But I knew that she was not carrying our child. I wanted to hug her and jump for joy in this, what should have been momentous occasion, but I only felt charity and love for her and the journey I knew she would be taking without us. I wanted so badly to take her by the hand, the same hand she offered me when requesting us to be the parents and help her find her true parents for her child.

Our relationship didn't last long, as it was important for her to spend her time and energy in finding the right parents. For the time we knew her, I felt a real connection to her through compassion for her journey. As we parted in the rain and drove home from our ice cream date with her, we felt unsettled with her request as we knew we weren't who she needed. The peace that followed was pure love for her and a prayer for her journey. Compassion came, in letting her go.

4)   "Be playfully wise."

Everyone has something to bring to the table in a relationship. Everyone carries a story with them, waiting to be shared and offered up for others to gravitate towards. We all have talents and ways that we can help others. Respect that of others and there will be little standing in your way of obtaining human connection.

When I think of that phrase, "be playfully wise", it makes me think about how we tend to focus more of our energy on our own stories, rather than creating a space for others to own theirs. We are wise to be a sounding board and soak in what people can enrich our lives with, and playfully wise to keep our attitude and connections fun and joyful. The human connection is more than just an exchange of stories, words and touch, it's an exchange of souls and the whole concept of humanity.

5)   "Listen, listen, listen."

Listening comes in several varieties: passive, selective, and active. Passive is where you hear it, but don't absorb what you are hearing. Selective is just that—you choose to hear what you want to hear. Lastly, there is active listening. This is the type of listening you should strive for in forming deep human connections. When you actively listen to someone, you hear them, you bring what they are saying into your heart, and then you engage. Engaging is seeking for empathy or finding that connection within their words. I will speak more on empathy later in the book.

Back to obtainability. Here I was a nursing student, with a whole new set of dreams settling in. I began to have a recurring dream during this time. I dreamt about a man who stood tall with confidence, his hands on his hips. He wore glasses and had the biggest, most beautiful smile I had ever seen. The dream haunted me, in a pleasant way. Who was this man I was dreaming of? What did this dream mean? I never saw his entire face or eyes, so I couldn't figure out who he was or why I was having this dream. One Friday, while in a lab class, my friend turned to me and whispered, "Hey, my brother is coming to town tonight. Would you want to go bowling with my husband, me, and my brother?" My first thought was "No, not really."

She had mentioned him before, when telling me about her family, but all I really knew was that he was two years younger than me and had just returned from his mission. I wasn't excited about another pity date. However, it was Friday night and I had just turned 23. What else was I going to do on a Friday at home with my parents? "Sure, why not?" was the only response I could come up with.

While I didn't know it at the time, he wasn't thrilled at the idea of our date, either. His sister had originally set him up with a different friend, who had cancelled that morning. She had shown him pictures of her friend and told him enough about her that he agreed to take her out. He had no interest in going on a blind date with someone he knew nothing about and had never seen before. But his sister had already asked me to come. Finally, after some prodding and begging, his mother blurted out, "Just go on the date. You don't have to marry the girl." Reluctantly, he got in the car and drove over to my house.

Neither one of us intended to create a meaningful human connection with each other. My main thought as I opened the door was, "Just get through this night with a smile on your face and it will all be over soon." His, flatteringly, was "Please be Paula, please be Paula."

Though I didn't see this connection going anywhere beyond this date, and neither did he, it ended up being one of the best dates I had ever been on. I laughed so hard the whole night that my abs got a great workout. Perhaps because neither of us were trying desperately to impress the other, we were willing to be fully ourselves. Authentic, real, with no ulterior motives. Needless to say, we had fun and I left that date much more impressed than when I first laid eyes on him.

After a few weeks of "phone dating," because he lived three hours away, we agreed to exchange pictures. When I got his picture in the mail, I nearly fell off my bed. IT WAS THE MAN OF MY DREAMS. It was a picture of him standing tall, resting his hands in fists on his hips. His posture was powerful and demanded respect. Then his smile melted you, softening the initially intimidating stance. He wore designer glasses (which I later found out he had borrowed from a friend because he doesn't need glasses). It was all of him, not just the pieces from my dreams. His eyes pierced my soul in that moment, and I knew he really was the man from my dreams. God had prepared me for this moment.

God wanted to be sure I recognized what was being created for me, knowing my heart was hard and that I wasn't interested in any attempt to form a strong human connection with anyone. All the sudden, marital bliss and happiness in companionship was obtainable.

In a matter of months, everything changed for me. I almost couldn't keep up with God's plan for me. We all face this during our early adulthood years. How do you keep up with what is good, right, and obtainable? Through faith, prayer, and scripture study. That's my answer at least. As I discussed earlier with scripture, God is a god of truth: He cannot lie. While we explore our life choices and experience them, we try to discover which is the best path to take, which direction is His plan for us, our best guide book is the scriptures. Making sure you have a relationship with Father in Heaven, God, or whatever your greater being may be, is key to understanding what is obtainable in life and your ultimate happiness through the journey of life.

Optimism

"The secret of change is to focus all of your energy not on fighting the old, but on building the new" – Socrates

Not all families are created equal. In fact, families are created in many different ways, through different people. If all families were created the same, many of us would miss out on the opportunity to learn and grow from those we were blessed to have met in our paths. We would also miss out on the opportunity to extend the arms of God to others and be blessed with their love in return.

Our son was 6 months old when we celebrated his adoption finalization as well as becoming an eternal family. We also blessed him in our church on our daughter's third birthday that Sunday. It was a large family celebration. My parents, my husband's parents, and some of our siblings and cousins were there, as were our son's birth father and birth mother, and grandparents from both sides. Our daughter's birth mother and her husband, our daughter's birth father and his wife and son, and her birth grandparents from both sides also attended. While the opportunity for "awkward" was definitely present, that is not at all how it felt. This was one of my favorite gatherings. It made me realize that there is no better way to celebrate than with family. Some of the family members were concerned that not everyone would feel welcomed or accepted into our family, but I went into the weekend with optimism. After all, for me, they ALL are family to us. Without all these amazing people, I would not be a mother.

My husband and I needed these children in our home, in our hearts, and in our lives. We are their parents. I am their mother.

Through open adoption, we have expanded our family and multiplied the love available to our children. For us, open adoption means open communication with all involved, invitations to family gatherings, inclusion in family reunions, vacations, and other important family events. We love all the people that make up our family.

Writing this book happened through many different stages of our adoption journey. I continued to write when I thought there would be an end to it. Then I realized that our story would never have an ending. (Don't worry, I will stop the story somewhere.) In fact, our story is still being written as I write this now. Throughout our story, there are mountains and valleys, ebbs and flows, optimistic views, and bleak pessimistic attitudes. This is what life is all about. How can we grow if we are not faced with challenges and failures along the way? But how I grow the most is from having an optimistic outlook of the other side, most of the time. The side of me that I haven't yet met. The other side of the mountain I climb each day. I don't know what lies ahead. I don't know where my journey will take me. What I do know is that my Savior, the son of God, walks next to me each step of the way.

Sometimes I have felt completely alone, as many people do amidst their trials. There is a poem called "Footprints in the Sand." This poem talks about the lonely path we feel we are taking in life. We sometimes see two set of footprints in the sand, and other times, the times when we feel like we just can't do it alone, there is only one set of footprints. By the end of the poem, we find out that when there was only one set of footprints, we weren't left on our own—that is when our Savior carried us.

With nursing school and the many other adventures, I had been on, I was already well on my way to some valuable life lessons about "making it" in life. Although becoming a nurse had not been my original plan, or second plan, or third plan, I knew that this was the Lord's plan for me at the time—and it was a better plan for me than I had dreamt of. And then I had that fateful first date with Carl. Four months after seeing his picture, I was blissfully married to Carl in the Logan, Utah Temple. At the time, twenty-three was considered old to be getting married in the culture of my faith. So, for me, I felt as though I had finally made it in life. I had my longed-for husband and was ready to start my adventure in motherhood. But remember how I talked about God being the true composer or author of my story, of all of our stories? Well, the change of direction my story took is testimony to that truth.

I had big dreams of having a large family long before marrying Carl. Little did I know that my plan of being a mother of seventeen little ones, with possibly a few sets of twins along the way, was not what the Lord had written for me. He was working on a completely different story, one that I would learn to love and appreciate years later.

It didn't take long for my 23-year-old newlywed self to become "baby hungry." If we were going to follow my plan to have as many children as I wanted to have, then we needed to get started. "I wasn't getting any younger," was my argument. Carl, however, was not ready. Having just started his schooling, and not being able to provide for a family, he was hesitant to jump into any family life with children.

So, I waited, not so patiently, for Carl to jump on the baby bandwagon with me. In the meantime, I worked as a pediatric nurse, caring for a handful of fragile little angels. These were God's children with special needs, who needed around-the-clock care. I was one of the blessed nurses that spent days and nights with my patients. They became such a big part of my life and heart. I would often tell myself, "If I can't be a mother of my own children, I will try my best to help other mothers with their children." These little angels I cared for truly became my children vicariously. I had also worked as a nanny for a little boy and his sister. These children were also becoming my children in my heart. However, I was still optimistic that we would be able to start a family of our own.

Two years after we were married, Carl applied for a job that would provide us with a much better income. We were at my niece's baby blessing when Carl whispered to me, "If I get this job, we can start having a family." I was overjoyed. My plan immediately reset to start your family and have lots of children. The optimism quickly turned to heartbreak when Carl did not get the job. My plans were put on hold yet again. By now, I had a total of eight boys and four girls in the flock of kids I was caring for through being a nanny and a nurse. They filled a portion of the void I felt in my heart. However, I had no clue as to the void my heart could truly experience. Then a year later, we finally decided to start a family. I was 26 and so ready. Over-ready really. *Seventeen children, here we go! It was possible, right?*

Why seventeen, you ask? Well, when I was a teenager, we played a game. Get a pencil and tie a string to the end of the pencil, just around the eraser. Once you have it secured, you hang it over the palm of your hand. Hold it there steadily until it begins to swing. When the pencil swings like a pendulum in a straight line, it means you are having a boy. When it swings in a circle, it's a girl. You let the pencil determine your motherly fate, and when it stops swinging, that's it. You're done. And I was naïve and believed the universe, speaking not through God, but through a pencil, would determine my fate as a mother. I totally got into this game, since I was so excited to be a mother someday. My pencil would swing twelve times in a circle and five in a straight line. Wow, seventeen kids, twelve girls and five boys. I was elated. Just to prove the theory right, I repeated this process several times, always with the same results. At least, that is what I remember. Talk about being a little overly optimistic about one's future.

While researching for this book, I studied my scriptures as a great source of solace. In search of stories of optimism, I found that the word optimism wasn't in the scriptures. Instead, the words "cheerfulness" and "hope" were found. Cheerfulness and hope. I was intrigued by those words and found it interesting that that is how the scriptures define optimism. Proverbs chapter 15 verse 13 reads, "A merry heart maketh a cheerful countenance: but by sorrow of the heart the spirit is broken." (KJV) A happy and optimistic heart comes from cheerfulness. How we view our trials and hardships, whether it be with cheerfulness or with sorrow, determines whether we approach obstacles with optimism or pessimism.

After a few months of trying and not getting pregnant, I became worried. My optimistic view of the large family I dreamt of was waning. I am not a patient woman, and I just knew there had to be something wrong. I had been battling some medical issues for quite some time, but nothing that should keep me from having a baby . . . so I thought. But in my gut, I just knew there was something wrong and I wasn't going to waste any more time waiting for a miracle.

Back to the movie I watched as a young girl, about the girl who danced in heaven, but was confined to a wheelchair on Earth. I thought to myself again, "That's me." All I ever wanted was to be a mother, and then I would soar through life the way the girl in the movie wanted to dance through life. All would be right in the world. But my trial on Earth had begun.

Each week in our church congregation, which was made up of young newlyweds, I'd hear yet another couple announcing their exciting news. They were having a baby. Week after week, another baby announcement. And week after week, my well-meaning friends would tell me, "Relax, it will happen for you too."

Those words pierced right through me like a hot knife. My thoughts immediately turned cold and sorrow filled my countenance. *"Oh, no worries, I'm relaxed. Can't you see how relaxed I am? Totally relaxed when every month I'm still not pregnant, not to mention all the medical issues I am enduring and the physical pain they cause. Yep, totally relaxed over here!"*

"Don't think about it, it will happen," they said.

"But how can you not think about getting pregnant when that is what you've wanted your whole life, and you're not getting pregnant?" I would think, mutter, or reply depending on my present desperation.

A little dramatic? Yep. I certainly was dramatic about it. By this point, I was considered the "grandma" of our congregation, especially since I had self-proclaimed myself the "official baby-holder." Although aching desperately to have a baby of my own, I thrived on holding others' babies and attempted to fill my empty arms with their children, if only for a moment. It helped, but the emptiness remained rooted deep inside.

I attempted to reach out in service, my arms preoccupying themselves with other mothers' joys. But my heart was as closed as I could force it shut. My soul was in a protective mode. Protecting me from continued disappointment when I faced each day without the announcement I so yearned for. I was nearly twenty-eight at the time—one of the oldest in our congregation—and I was really good at holding babies. I was surrounded by them, yet none of them were mine. It was all I wanted: a baby, a pregnancy, a family to create. The dreams of having seventeen children were slipping away and my cheerfulness and optimism disappeared with it. I hadn't yet learned how to live an open life with open arms.

In the Book of Mormon, Another Testament of Jesus Christ, I found this scripture to put the feelings I was having into some perspective. In the book of 2 Nephi, chapter 31 verse 20, it reads: "Wherefore, ye must press forward with a steadfastness in Christ, having a perfect brightness of hope and a love of God and of all men. Wherefore, if ye shall press forward feasting upon the word of Christ, and endure to the end, behold, thus saith the Father: Ye shall have eternal life."

In one sense, life happens whether we are passive participants or live it wholeheartedly. Each day we move on physically. This scripture reminds us that we must move forward with "a perfect brightness of hope" to truly live. In other words, press forward, not just move on inevitably. When Thomas Edison's mother received a note from his teacher that said, "Your son is addled. We won't let him come to school anymore," she chose to move forward with a brightness of hope. Instead of reading the words on the page to her child, she told him that the note read, *"Your child is a genius. This school is too small for him and doesn't have enough good teachers for training him. Please teach him yourself."* (http://www.videoinspiration.net/blog/famous-story-determination/)

Edison, who went on to invent the lightbulb, among many other achievements, was not given the opportunity to fail due to a bleak outlook. His mother's optimistic view of her son's potential, along with her "perfect brightness of hope," led him to be successful. He could have been brought to a screeching halt if told what the note really said. Instead, his mother instilled in him the will to continue and press forward with cheerfulness and hope, regardless of his obstacles. If only we all could be like Thomas Edison's mother. I wish I could say that I was as courageous as Edison's mother during a time of heartbreak. She was so quick to alter those pessimistic words into an optimistic view of life for her son. I wish I could have seen my trials the same way she did while I was in the thick of it all. But we can only learn and move forward from past mistakes.

As I have evolved through my life's experiences, my optimistic goggles have grown thicker. Learning to sit with my trials and see them as opportunities and not obstacles has opened my eyes to being able to be more optimistic. That mountain to climb is an adventure not a burden. I'm excited by the stumbling blocks I face, I know in the end I will have learned and hopefully become a better version of myself because of them. C.S. Lewis said, "Experience is the most brutal of teachers, but you learn, my God, do you learn". It is from embracing our experiences that we evolve into the new person each day brings us. You can either have an optimistic outlook and know that the person you will become is capable of greater human connection with self and others or you can look at your trials as far too great a feat and repeat the past without broadening your strength of self. After all the ultimate goal to evolve ourselves is to be able to have something to give in our human connections. You cannot give water from an empty pail.

Our open adoptions have been the greatest teacher for learning to be optimistic. Looking at another's soul from a raw perspective force you to be optimistic about an open relationship with them. In all the moments when we have needed to be open with our families, both bio and adoptive, I feel as though we have to look to the good and reach for positivity for the relationships to thrive. Hiding emotions and thoughts doesn't offer the connections needed to teach our children to love all people and be optimistic about their future as human beings. That's what it all comes down to, its teaching generations to be kind and decent human beings making connections for a more optimistic future.

CHAPTER 2

O"P"en

"But if we hope for that we see not, then do we with patience wait for it." – Romans 8:25 (KJV)

"Come unto me, all ye that labour and are heavy laden, and I will give you rest. Take my yoke upon you....and ye shall find rest unto your souls. For my yoke is easy and my burden is light." – Matthew 11:28-30(KJV)

Trials are made lighter when we give it all up to Him. When we stop worrying about everything that pertains to us because we cannot change a single thing through worrying. Rather, in prayers, He takes up our burdens because He truly cares for us.

I have always been a huge advocate for adoption, both before and after going through the experience personally. Although it involves a long and grueling process of interviews, paperwork, and classes, adoption is WELL WORTH IT in the end. I can tell you that at the end of that process, if the FBI, state authorities, Church authorities, and every other background check person didn't find us fit to be parents, then I don't know who would be. Learning to persevere, to look at things from a different perspective, and to have patience in my trials has helped lead me to the life I now know . . . a much better life than I had naively designed for myself.

 Paula Kanani Weeks

Persevere

"Success is not the absence of failure; it's the persistence through failure." – Aisha Tyler

"Charity suffereth long." What does it mean to "suffereth long?" Is there a need for agony, and to what extent do you need to agonize? Does each day or task need to be so difficult? I don't believe so. It certainly feels like it sometimes, though. There is a phrase that says, *"if it were easy, it isn't worth it."* This is also true in adoption. It is never a simple walk in the park, and you may not appreciate the benefits of the pain until you have the joy of experiencing the rewards. At which point you could come to the realization that all the suffering, or more appropriately the perseverance and pushing through the pain, was worth it.

There was a study focusing on delayed gratification done in the late 1960s by a professor at Stanford University, Walter Mischel, named the Stanford Marshmallow Experiment. Each child in the study was given one marshmallow and then left in the room, alone, for fifteen minutes. If they didn't eat the one marshmallow in that time, they were given another one, a more rewarding treat. Follow up research showed that the children who persevered and waited for the greater reward were more likely to be more success-ful in life. These children had better test scores, better health, and better outcomes in life. I am sure the fifteen-minute wait for the greater reward was no small task. The children likely experienced a little suffering. Possibly, they agonized over the sweetness of the marshmallow, their mouths salivating, and their noses tickled with the sugary smell. But if they were willing to persevere, how much sweeter the reward! With adoption, there are times when the marshmallow staring back at us is the potential of a child, or even just the idea of children. When the wait is over, how much greater is the reward, how much sweeter the treat, for the time earned spent waiting.

So how does charity play a part in persevering through your journey? Charity is the pure love of Christ. Christ suffered a great deal for the greatest reward, eternal life, and salvation, and it wasn't even for Himself: He suffered pain, mocking, even death, for us. As our Savior and Redeemer, He suffered for us all. Above all, He exemplifies perseverance.

We, too, must show charity to others as we persevere if we are to create authentic, lasting human connections. In 1st Peter chapter 5, elders are asked to feed God's flock. When we feed one another, either with food or in spirit, we cannot have judgment for them. Compassion and empathy must ensue, regardless of the path their journey has taken.

About 8 months after our adoption papers were completed, my husband and I were finally contacted by a birthmother, via email. This was our very first contact from anyone regarding the possibility of becoming parents. We exchanged emails for a little more than a week before she requested to meet with us. Our case worker was unavailable when this birthmother wanted to meet, and we didn't know how to proceed.

The birthmother lived two hours away and she had found us on the internet on her own, rather than through our agency. She told us she was having twin girls. My stomach jumped at the idea of twins. Two little blessings of joy! Four hands to hold, four feet to tickle, twenty toes to play "This little piggy." I had always thought I would have twins, or at least I had hoped for twins. I was eager to move forward and find out more. The thought of my first "marshmallow" was making my mouth water. I wanted to devour this treat: twins! How could it possibly get better?

We arranged to go meet the birthmother personally, driving the two hours to her hometown to take her out for ice cream. We wanted to keep the first visit casual and friendly, to make sure she was comfortable. The evening was pleasant, relaxed, as if we had met up with an old friend. Conversation was light, with laughter. She told us what she was doing in her life and shared her hobbies, her likes, and her dislikes. We shared a little about us, but our focus was on getting to know her and the baby. That's right . . . the (one) baby.

Unfortunately, she had mixed up this pregnancy with the last one she had where she had placed twin boys for adoption a few years back. She was having one little girl. It didn't bother me much whether it was one baby or two. If it was one baby, two babies, or ten, I just wanted to be a mother. I was simply grateful for the prospect of a child. It became very clear over the visit, however, that we needed more information.

At the time of our meeting, she had yet to meet with a counselor, let alone a doctor. She had recently been in jail, but having placed children twice before, she knew the routine. Find a family, contact them, share the news that they were going to be parents, and then proceed with the pregnancy. There were many unanswered questions hovering in our minds, and we had many concerns. She agreed to contact her doctor and meet with an agency.

Our visit was nearing the end, and night was slowly creeping in when she reached over and gently placed her hands on mine saying, "I want you to be the parents." Me, a mom. Finally! My stomach jumped and then quickly dropped as if I were on a rollercoaster. The excitement of hearing those words left as quick as it came. Why was I not thrilled? I couldn't wait for those words to cross the lips of a birthmother! But the sudden emptiness I felt was undeniable. Something wasn't right, and clearly the Lord knew. Had that not been the case, I would have been just as elated as I had expected to be.

We dropped her off at her apartment and left with a verbal agreement to stay in touch and continue to pray with her for the confirmation of the right answer as we developed a relationship with her. The bond developed between a birthmother and adoptive mother, early on, is an important step in the open adoption experience. But as we drove away, the two-hour car ride was silent. I looked at Carl and asked, "Are you excited?" We both kind of shrugged our shoulders. What were these emotions? Why the empty feeling inside?

Adoption is sacred. It's a tender yet messy process. In totality, it is ultimately a beautiful experience. There is no room for judging other people's choices or their paths in life, there can only be room for charity. We suffer with them, and we love them because we are not better than they are. As it is stated in the Bible, in 1 Corinthians chapter 13, "Charity is kind."

We decided to persevere in our journey with a prayerful and charitable heart. Although it was painful not to feel the joy I expected with this birthmother when she requested us to be the parents of her unborn child, Carl and I both developed a deep love for her courage to do what she thought was best for her child. I prayed for her. I prayed for her child. I prayed for what was right and deeply wanted her to be guided to the right parents, because we were not them.

In the human connection, we persevere through the process it takes to become connected. Human connection can be messy and full of, well, humans. Nobody is perfect and therefore the connections take charitable love and perseverance to obtain. If you desire connection, which we all do, we must allow for the imperfectness of it all to play a part in the growth of it.

We connected on a superficial level with this particular birth mom, for the short time that we knew her. It wasn't necessary to persevere or even pursue a deep, meaningful connection at that time. Sure, we could have stayed connected and worked at that relationship, but it was more important for all of us to go our separate ways. Not all connections or even relationships will last, and that's ok. Energies are more vital for genuine connections in our lives. Circle yourself with those who can lift you up in this life on earth. Persevere in those relationships that can be built on honest to goodness authentic connections.

Perspective

"Train yourself to find the blessing in everything" – author unknown

Life is hard: Trials are harder still. But isn't that the reason why we are here? We are meant to face our trials head on and emerge victorious, having learned from them, and become ready for bigger challenges. All trials serve as a tool for refining us. It's called the refiner's fire. In the final stage of gold production, it goes through a process of refinement in the fire. This is where all the impurities are removed from the gold. Our trials are a refiner's fire in our lives. They help us to become more pure and closer to the person we are meant to be as we burn away the dross. We can gain knowledge and wisdom through the life lessons we learn in our trials.

In verse 10 of 1 Peter, chapter 5, we read, "But the God of all grace, who hath called us unto his eternal glory by Christ Jesus, after that ye have suffered a while, make you perfect, establish, strengthen, settle you." What blessings there are for us after the refinement process! To be perfect in Christ, to gain strength in Him, and to be settled. Allowing our weaknesses to be sloughed off in the refinement process helps us find strength as we grow stronger from our trials. What a joy to find proof of this process in the scriptures.

Brene Brown, a research professor at the University of Houston and 5-time #1 best-selling author, talks a lot about how we live in fear, which keeps us from finding true belonging or the human connection in our own lives. We have a tendency to keep our pain and fear in dark secret places, rather than owning those feelings and allowing them to be a voice with purpose as we form mean- ingful human connections. I see this often when interacting with people in the adoption community. When we turn away from oth- ers and convince ourselves that we are the only one who expe- rience particular pain, we disconnect from others. This in turn pulls us apart rather than bringing people together.

We humans also tend to be more concerned with our own per- spective rather than taking a moment to see things from someone else's point of view.

The importance of perspective was reinforced to me on a hike with our oldest two children. My little children were more than eager to be outdoors on what we called our adventure hikes. We would give them things to look for, and they would enthusiasti- cally search for the items as if they were on a treasure hunt.

While on a particular hike, I noticed two trees standing near one another. One was standing tall and straight, reaching up to the sky. It was hard not to notice its majestic glory. The other was crooked and nearly blocked our path. I was so intrigued with the two opposing trees. At first, I wanted to be like the first tree, standing tall and beautiful—she looked nearly perfect. On the other hand, her sister tree had been through a bit more of a refin- er's fire. The trunk was wider and sturdier, and bent into a curve parallel to the ground. It didn't sway in the wind like the first.

We stopped to rest and sat on the crooked tree. She held all four of us with her strength and power. Her sturdy trunk and branches, which nearly touched the ground, didn't crumble at the weight of us. I imagined that if I would climb the straight and tall tree, she would bend with the weight, not having the thick trunk and steady branches that the other did.

That's when I realized I wanted to be like the second tree. Although the tall tree was beautiful and had a power in her own right, the second tree was stronger and able to better serve others. She grew this way because of the trials and forceful winds that gave her her form. She bent and stretched in the refining, but grew a stronger base, deeper roots, and sturdier bark to help her withstand the difficult times. She carried her own beauty and was able to serve our needs.

Most would see the perfectly tall tree and want to emulate her grace and elegance. However, should we not be more like the crooked tree, allowing our trials to bend us at times, only to come out greater and stronger from it? Perspective is key in this example.

Gaining perspective doesn't mean there aren't negatives in your life. For example, there is no happy ending for infertility. It's a pretty finite journey and the sting of pain will always be there. I don't mean to sound gloom and doom, but the truth is that, years later, it still hurts knowing I will never bear a child. But it is perfectly normal and okay to feel this way. Nowhere does it say that you have to be totally okay with your pain of infertility in order to have a happy ending in parenthood. While I now have three beautiful children through adoption, and have made peace with my infertility, the pain is still there and always will be.

We definitively learned that having a family in the traditional sense wasn't going to happen for us near the end of summer in 2005. After many tests, a few surgeries/procedures, and several doctors, I sat with Carl at our kitchen table as we listened to the doctor on the line tell us, "I do not see you being able to have children biologically. I'm sorry." It's over, you can't have kids, stop trying. Wait, what? Could you repeat that? Are you saying that my plans of being a mother are not going to happen? Not my favorite phone call for sure. Truthfully, not the best way to deliver such heavy news, either. Not only was my body dealing with painful cysts, lichen sclerosus, and other ailments (which don't necessarily cause infertility, just a lot of pain), but my husband had no sperm count. Our future for parenthood was bleak, at best. IVF (invitro fertilization), AI (artificial insemination), and other modern medicine options for infertility really weren't a possibility for us. We even considered donor sperm and surrogacy. It just didn't feel right for us. God closed that door for us pretty quickly after much pondering and prayer. But how was I supposed to "dance through life" and share all this love I had with all the children I dreamt of? What was next, adoption?

In October 2005, we went on a cruise. We called it our "get away from it all" trip because we needed a shift in perspective. As everyone knows, your problems and worries disappear while you are basking in the sun on a ship in the middle of the ocean. Right? NOT. However, it did help us recalibrate, table things for a bit, and get away.

It was a good decision to take time for ourselves, even if it was hard to shift my perspective at first. The questions began to flow like rain. Why can't my plans just be? Why can't I have what I want? Why is being a mother, a righteous desire, being taken away from me? Isn't this why we are here? To have forever families. I was lost in this sea of questions with no real answers on the horizon.

Regardless, upon our return from our getaway vacation, we decided to move into the next chapter of our lives and pursue adoption wholeheartedly.

Adoption was an easy answer for me, and thankfully, it was for Carl as well. In fact, I told Carl I wanted to adopt early on in our marriage. When I was a nursing student, another dream I had was to be a traveling nurse and practice nursing in third world countries while volunteering in orphanages. I dreamt of adopting children from there and being the mother I always wanted to be. So, our dreams of having a family shifted its focus and we headed in that direction.

We started the paperwork, and by paperwork, I mean a mountain of documents meant to prove we could be worthy, safe, and loving parents. It was a daunting task. The paperwork required us to expose every detail, making us completely vulnerable as we shared our most intimate lives with perfect strangers. I would spend hours preparing the house for a spotless and tidy inspection with every cupboard locked and every outlet covered. Don't get me wrong, I had no problem in preparing my house for a safe and loving environment. Cleaning is therapeutic for me. On the other hand, being constantly asked how I plan to raise my children and discipline them, or how my childhood was and how that would influence me as a mother, became quite the test. We answered questions like, "Would you consider a child from a mother on drugs? A mother who drank alcohol or who smoked cigarettes?"

How do you answer that? I didn't care what baby we were blessed with, but I was also a "mother in waiting" who didn't do drugs, or smoke, or drink alcohol, and especially wouldn't have while pregnant. The questions continued with brutal truth. Do you want a boy, or a girl, or twins, or more? Would you accept a biracial baby or baby of another ethnicity?

In my early plans, I had wanted a boy first, to be the big brother to his sisters and brothers. Or maybe twins first, a boy and a girl. But did it really matter? God was in charge, not me. It would be His plan, not mine. Then it hit me: when couples talk about having a baby and try to get pregnant, do they ask these questions of each other? Would it matter? You get what you get and celebrate the joy of having a family. We don't get to pick and choose what child we get, through pregnancy or adoption.

As an adoptive mother now, I see things from a different perspective than when I was in the middle of filling out papers. I have found that when you are "choosing" what you will accept, what you are actually choosing is to love unconditionally. When all is said and done, there are birthmothers who find themselves with a choice. What I want birthmothers to know is that, when the choice is made to place your sweet little ones in the arms of another, it doesn't matter how you got to this choice, and it doesn't matter why you made this choice. All that matters is that there is an unconditional love for these babies and what is best for them. This is the same love I have developed for birthmothers, birthfathers, and their families. It's about what is best for baby and baby's first parents. And as I write this, my babies are no longer babies, so it's what is best for their whole life, as babies, toddlers, children and then teens, until they become independent in their own right.

I read a saying once that seemed to sum up my feelings about the entire adoption paperwork process. In big, bold subway art letters, it read, "Just breathe and fill out the next form." I was drowning in paper forms and emotions, but it was necessary, so I followed the saying's advice. I just kept breathing and filling out the next form.

Finally, the day came when we were done with the required paperwork and it was time to put in our application and move forward with the new plan . . . not mine to begin with . . . but a much better plan for me. Our paperwork was finalized, the home study done, and we were APPROVED. It was October 2005, nine months before our first miracle.

I thought our efforts to get pregnant were a rough time. Little did I know what I would face in the next nine months after we became official adoptive parents in waiting or what some call "paper pregnant". Many of my loving friends and family tried to be supportive in their own way. "Now that your paperwork for adoption is in, you're going to get pregnant," and "You can relax now and maybe you will get pregnant," they said. But the amount of relaxation that would be needed to calm my nerves doesn't exist in this lifetime. I did still hold out hope for that flock of seventeen ducklings, though. It happened with others, why not me? "It's going to happen in no time, you're a good-looking couple," they said, "You'll be picked very soon," they said. But whose plan was this anyhow? Did the way we look really influence when God wanted us to have children? Was the fact that we were approved have any bearing on God's plan. Well, in fact, yes to the latter question. God has a plan, but we still have our agency to choose how we live this life. And we chose to put in our paperwork and wait to be adoptive parents. Once we made that choice, then we put our faith in God on how it would play out. Each week I would check my email and wait by the phone, anticipating that precious moment. The moment when we would get "the news." Each week, there was disappointment and difficulties.

We knew we couldn't have kids biologically, but I was still in pain, both physically and emotionally. I pushed forward with as much of a smile as I could muster up, all while seeing counselors and doctors to try to resolve some of my other medical concerns. I cried myself to sleep often. We finally had a plan, but we didn't have a clue as to when or what or how things would manifest themselves. My faith wavered, A LOT. Depression was becoming a hinderance to my happiness and "dance through life."

Sundays at church continued to be especially hard, as more and more families announced their growing families. I would sit in the back of the chapel and try to hide my tears. I'd also roll my eyes whenever someone would apologize for crying because they were "pregnant" or "just had a baby" and were therefore "emotional." Was I not allowed to be emotional too? Because I certainly wasn't pregnant, and I hadn't recently had a baby. Carl was serving in a leadership calling at the time. He sat on the stand while I sat alone in the congregation, playing the "grandma" role, and loving on all those beautiful babies and children that surrounded me when I could emotionally handle it.

One Sunday was particularly difficult for me. After our sacrament meeting, I walked up to Carl, who could see my facial expression throughout the meeting from his vantage point up on the stand. I was looking for comfort and expected him to tell me I was justified in crying and being "emotional," Instead, Carl lovingly wrapped his arms around me while I cried, "when will it be my turn," and shared these . . . attitude-adjusting words. He said, "I love you and I will always be here for you, but I cannot support your sour attitude towards your friends' happiness." Here I was, so focused on myself and how everyone should feel sorry for me and justify my tears, while my dear friends (whom I am so grateful to for sticking with me through my bad attitude) were relishing in their joys and the exciting news of their growing families. This experience changed the way I looked at my trials and how I was connecting or not connecting with my friends. It was still hard, but I was able to endure it "better" than I had. With this shift in perspective, I was able to turn around and open my arms to their happiness without denying my own struggles. It was an eye-opening moment that gave me an open perspective to what later would prove valuable in open adoption. Having a loving perspective of other's joys or trials and being able to support them through it all, is one way to allow for human connections to be made. Everyone has a story, everyone struggles, everyone has joys they wished to share. Your outward perspective for others brings a whole new world of human connection. You're not focusing on yourself but directing your energies for the other's well-being. This was important in open adoption because having an unconditional loving perspective of our birth families as humans and not just those who brought us children, brought us all closer together. This connection creates an environment for our children to grow in confidence of their own identity. One simply cannot have an open mind or perspective when trying to embrace openness while raising children in an open adoption environment. The word "open" alone explains this. As our relationships in our open adoptions have evolved, I am able to see everyone's perspectives through the many conversations we have. In fact, as

I edit this book we are spending the week in Florida with Zander's grandparents, twelve years after placement. Perspective of how open adoption can work has naturally grown into what it is today.

After stepping back and realizing I was not "enduring well," I found a way to shift my perspective on my situation and have a little fun with it. I posted some of my thoughts on my blog, and this is what came out.

"I have been thinking a lot about our "paper pregnancy" versus a "belly pregnancy." Let me just share with you a few of my thoughts...you have been warned. Please remember, I have never been pregnant, and so my comparisons are from what I hear it's like. Please give me grace."

*** When we fill out our paperwork and finally turn it into our caseworker***...*seeing that little blue line saying "pregnant" (you know, the little pee stick)*

*** Our first interview with the caseworker and agency***... *The first visit to the doctors confirming the pregnancy.*

*** Preparing our profile; scrapbook pages, letter to the birthparents, and web profile***...*sharing first ultrasound picture.*

*** Home study***...*decorating the nursery. (The home study is where our caseworker comes into our home to make sure our home is safe for a child; outlet covers, cupboard locks, fire extinguishers, smoke and CO2 alarms, safe neighborhood, age of roof, and where the new baby will be sleeping.)*

*** Waiting for the background checks to come back from the state and FBI***...*getting bigger and not necessarily* *enjoying the body changes, but embracing the beauty of life being created.*

** **Food cravings**...Food cravings (It goes without saying that emotional eating plays a role in the creation of family no matter how that looks)*

** **Getting the letter that we are approved**...Hearing the heartbeat; it's actually for real now.*

** **The nauseating wait**...nausea, throwing up, peeing all day, uncomfortable sitting down, getting up, can't see my feet, wish I could still do sit ups, backaches; you get the idea.*

** **Hearing from our birthparents, waiting for baby to come**...going into labor; some pain, short times of rest, then more pain, the blessed epidural.*

** **The birth of our baby**...the birth of the baby.*

Open adoption takes on many faces. The concept of open adoption began more than 50 years ago when birth moms were able to choose the families their children would go to. Before this time, a child put up for adoption was taken from their first mothers at birth and cared for by nursing staff until an unknown adoptive family was able to take the baby home and assume the role of parents. The concept changed when it was realized that this "break-up" wasn't doing birth mom or baby any good psychologically.

We had toyed with the idea of "open adoption" after hearing briefly about it in the support groups our agency provided. It was a newer concept among our agency, and we were uncertain about how it would work and what the process was. How would our perspective need to change to make it work? I had always liked the idea and was a little more open to the idea of open adoption. I imagined that if I were an adoptee, then I would want to know where I came from, whose traits I carried and what my birth parents were like. Carl wasn't so sure. He felt that we needed to be able to move on in our lives with our family, and that maybe it was best to allow a clean break after placement. Perhaps it would allow the birth mothers, birth fathers, and their families to move on as well.

However, as we have experienced our adoption journey, our perspectives shifted and we have come to understand that openness was and is so much better for our families.

In fact, the night Carl and I met Jerica, [the birthmother of our first child,] he said to me, "if she chooses us, we have to be open with them. We can't take this little girl away from them." This shocked me to hear from him, but I was on board. It was a decision that changed our lives in a way I never considered.

What was open adoption, truly? What did that look like for us, for them, and for our child? The only things we knew about open adoption at that point were that we'd send pictures back and forth, there'd be occasional meetings with birthparents and families, and of course, letters. I liked the idea of an open relationship; I want my children to embrace who they are and love where they came from. But was I really going to be a mother? Were we going to add another family to our little family of soon-to-be three? How was this all going to look for all parties involved? Would it be like the beautiful tall tree that majestically grew without any imperfections? Naturally that was the perspective we initially hoped for. Nobody likes confrontation, or challenges within a relationship. Was that realistic though? Would we feel disappointed, like we had with the first birthmother we were contacted by? No. As with any valuable relationship that is built on honesty and love, there will be hardships. There will be conflicts that need to be resolved through communication and having an open perspective of everyone's view.

It's an odd feeling to meet a birthmother who could potentially be carrying your child, and yet that baby is still not yours. And unlike our experience with the first birthmother, we had met with, we had a strong impression that this was our baby.

Long before meeting Jerica, I prayed hard for our adoption story to be hand-crafted and specially made for us. I wanted our story to be unique. A selfish request? Maybe. But that was what my heart desired. And I knew God was listening because of the many opportunities before that He had created for my life. So, I asked.

And God prepared us, just as he'd prepared me to recognize Carl, tall stature, big smile, glasses, and all, from my dream.

You see, I was born to a military father. Halfway through his career, he was stationed on a beautiful island in Hawaii, and that is where I was born. I am not Hawaiian, nor is my family, but it was still a special part of who I am since my own beginnings were there. In fact, I am daughter number four, and the only child of seven to be born in Hawaii.

The night we met Jerica, one of the first things she and her family told us was that this little baby growing inside her belly was "grown in Hawaii." Shortly after learning of her pregnancy, Jerica's family went on vacation to Hawaii. They decided to stay on the island for the remainder of her 10th grade school year, and nearly the rest of her pregnancy. Although not born there, our little baby girl grew strong in her birth mom's womb with island foods and island air. On the very same island I was born on. That was an answer to my prayers. This is how God told us and confirmed that this baby was to be ours to love and nurture.

We still needed to meet the birthfather and his family. We were asked if we would meet with them the next day, for interview number two. I don't mean to be so casual with the word "interview," but that is how you feel when in a face-to-face meeting with birth parents. You are being considered and judged. *Will they be good parents? Is this the right decision for my child? Can they really be the best for my baby?*

We walked away from Jerica's family home with a powerful feeling of unconditional love for her. After meeting with our daughter's first family and spending the night with some friends that lived nearby, we had a lot to consider, and yet we hadn't even been "chosen" yet. That night was a sleepless night, imagining all things baby, and how we would move forward in this relationship. The next morning, we drove a short distance to the birthfather's home, where we were greeted by Jeff and his mother. Their home was beautifully decorated with his mother's hand-crafted talents. They were pleasant upon our arrival, but the mood was a little different. A little more somber and quieter, with a heaviness I can't explain. The conversation started out similar to the one we'd had the night before: "What are your hobbies? Where do you work? What are your plans for the future?" This went back and forth for a few minutes, and then it got real. "How do you feel about adoption?" we asked Jeff. He wasn't as excited as we hoped he would be. I am not sure Jeff, and his mother were big fans of us at the time. Our being there was an invasion of their privacy and wishes for this little baby girl, and they weren't convinced we were the best choice for his baby girl. He grew up with two sets of parents and thought this normal and sufficient. Losing this baby to perfect strangers was not Jeff's idea of what was best for his daughter, nor his mother's wishes.

We left their home with a weird mix of uncertainty, but also complete confidence that this baby was still to be ours. While we didn't see eye-to-eye in the matter and the emotions were different, we still walked away feeling optimistic about this adoption. It's difficult to really explain how you can have polar opposite emotions exist in the same space. Not only was Jeff uncertain, but his mother also had some concerns of her own. How could she agree to have her grandchild go to some strangers, rather than family? Who were we to come in and tell them we were the best choice for this little baby girl?

How could we warm their hearts to the idea that we now were considering an open adoption? It wasn't something we talked about in that meeting. We weren't planning it all out of how open we wanted to be at that point, as Carl and I still had concerns about an open adoption. Would our children grow up and love their birthparents more than us? Wouldn't they be the cool ones since we had to discipline and set the ground rules for our family? Would birth mom and birth dad want them back? I think every adoptive parent wonders that. We needed to consider our child's needs and what was best for her, and we knew nothing about how to raise a child in an open adoption, or even how to raise a child at all; this was our first. At this point it was one day at a time, one breath at a time. On this day, we were just glad to get through the face-to-face meetings with some grace and a smile on our faces.

A few days later…we got "the call." Jerica told us she would like for us to be the adoptive parents. Words cannot describe what we really felt in that moment. It was a mixture of relief, joy and excitement. What should we do next?

In our case, we went shopping. That's the answer to every other stressor, right? Get your mind off things and go shopping. We bought all the little girl things we thought we would need for a baby that was to come to us any day. Diapers, formula, bottles, pacifiers, blankets, and of course the cutest little girl clothes we could find.

In the meantime, there was still this other birthmother who had chosen us. How were we going tell her she was not carrying our baby? We knew it wasn't the right choice to adopt her baby, but why couldn't I have both? Yes, I can be a little selfish at times. If I could, I would take them all. I couldn't be that selfish, so unfortunately for us, we had to part ways with her. We had to tell her exactly that: "You are carrying someone else's baby." Someone else is praying just as hard as we have been for the opportunity to start their own family.

I bawled for the loss of that baby. In infertility, even the loss of a potential adoption is a very heavy loss in a mama's heart. Although we are very aware of the fact that a baby is not ours until the adoption is finalized, loss is loss. But the loss of baby C didn't negate our joy of our baby who was coming soon.

We finally got to announce our news, just like so many of my family and friends had done before us. It was our turn to shout from the rooftops, "WE ARE GONNA BE PARENTS." We began to plan her life and prepare our homecoming with her. We spoke with

Jerica almost daily, making sure she was ok and handling things well. We prepared care packages and bought gifts for Jerica to have as keepsakes. I was good at this part. I wanted to be best friends with Jerica and have her be at peace with her decision. I wanted her to know that we were going to raise her little girl in the most loving home that she so deserved. I wanted Jeff and his mom to know that we were worthy of being their little girl's parents. Could they love us enough to accept us?

One evening, while out celebrating with some friends, we got a call from Jerica. She said, "Jeff has decided he doesn't want to sign the relinquishment papers." Not a call you ever want to get. I was silent. What was I supposed to say? "Ok, well, maybe next time, thanks for considering us?" Nope, I had nothing to say. I hung up the phone and bawled my eyes out. What were we going to do? I was supposed to be a mother, and Carl was supposed to be a father. Did we have to call all those family and friends back and tell them, "Just kidding, we are not going to be parents?" But something inside me said, "It's all going to be ok. That is your baby." Was I arrogant for thinking that, or was that faith in God's plan? This was a plan I was on board with and ready for. I tried to hold on to that faith, just to get me through the days, but the uncertainty of the outcome still hurt. Not having any control over a situation is the worst; it's almost too difficult to bear.

That next weekend, when the baby was supposed be born and in my arms, we were praying, and asking family to pray, as we not-so-patiently waited for a final decision to be made. While we were praying and waiting, the baby was still in Jerica's belly. She knew she needed to wait, and I am so grateful for her patience to this day. Jeff's family was going to have a family meeting about how to raise this baby between birthmom and birthdad, who both still had high school to finish. What was their next step? There were two families that needed to discuss what to do, and how time would be spent with their little girl. In all honesty, we weren't a part of the picture at this point.

As we prayed and waited, I approached with situation with the perspective that, even if this baby didn't come to my arms, I loved her and wanted what was best for her. I loved her birthmother and birthfather and wanted them to be happy and be able to have everything they wanted. I feared we had just lost this little girl, when I had just passed on another baby days before. But I feared with faith. I had to dig for the feeling, since my human mind can only see what was happening right in front of me. In the end, though the fear was there, I still knew, through faith, this baby was ours. Yes, two heavy emotions can share the same space.

This was a scary rollercoaster, for sure. Waiting for that one call, the one that announces your potential for parenthood, is a difficult part of adoption for me, but when that call comes, all the wait is worth it. Monday morning rolled around and it was a few days past baby's due date. I am convinced that baby girl was up in heaven waiting patiently for all parties to get on board with God's plan. She knew what the plan was, and she was ok waiting to come. Then we got "the call" again. Jerica, on the other end of the phone, said, "Jeff's family met and he has decided to agree to place baby girl for adoption. He won't dispute it anymore." What a sigh of relief and answer to our prayers. Jerica was to be induced the next day.

Our perspective of how open adoption would be was fluid. It changed every day, sometimes in every moment. There were too many players in the game, too many people's emotions to consider, too many perspectives that needed to weigh in on decisions to not be open-minded about what an open adoption would look like for us. Open adoption is not a one and done experience. We had to view it as an organic and everchanging journey. Our perspective in life should be the same when considering the human connection. We cannot always walk into a situation with an attitude of "my way or the highway." There are too many variables to consider, and we need to allow for growth, change, and increased understanding from all parties.

Patience

"Sometimes it's hard to see the rainbow when there's been endless days of rain" – Christina Greer

Put down the umbrella, I thought; let the rain fall and wash away the sorrow. See through it with a sight that will only allow the beauty in. Days and days of rain, often running into my own tears, unable to know which is which, straining to see through wet lashes. Why do we let the rain interfere with the rays of color pushing their way to us through the clouds? Waiting for the rainbow to shine can be a test of patience when being drenched with rain.

I love a great surprise. In gift giving, in gift receiving, in vacation planning, and all the above. If my husband picked me up one day and swept me away to a getaway island for a week without any mental prep time, I'd be thrilled. It's the hopeless romantic in me. However, I have learned that not everyone loves a surprise. Take my husband, for example. He likes the anticipation that leads up to the occasion. The wait and the buildup to the grand adventure. When he prepares to undertake a hunting or fishing trip, he starts to tie hooks and pack his bags weeks before the trip. He carefully chooses his gear and the proper attire for the appropriate trip far ahead. On the other hand, I pack my things at the last minute, and I may change my mind about a certain outfit or item I want to take along even at the final minute.

When it comes to adoption, I have had to learn to look at it like the way he prepares for a hunting trip, with emphasis placed on enjoying the anticipation and preparing for what is about to come. While I love a great surprise, the fear of the unknown is still there. My main frustration is that I have no control over the timing or any knowledge of when the trip will happen or be completed. However, the lesson learned is that it's about the joy in the journey, not about when or how the journey will end.

How can we obtain that joy in the journey? What positive attributes can be found during the wait for any long-awaited journey?

Patience.

Patience means to be able to wait for something without frustration. The waiting game sometimes is inevitable and will happen regardless, "without frustration" is where true patience lies. Not easy to do, but a valuable character trait to aspire to have within ourselves. Any character traits we learn along our journey are virtuous for our beings, our souls, and of course valuable in connecting with others.

Patience is obtained from an attitude of acceptance that there is inevitably a wait in all good things. There are interludes composed in songs, intermissions between act one and act two in plays, a rest before the grand conclusion. With our first child, the wait was nearly exactly nine months after our approval went through, although we did not know about her until two weeks before she was born. There was a lot of radio silence in those nine months, many moments when the canvas rested between colors being splayed across the page. Moments when not knowing about her were agonizing. The wait for our second adopted child, our son, was a much longer wait than we had with our first daughter. This wait was about a year and a half from start to finish with our son. When we started the adoption process with our son, his birth parents chose us five months before his birth. They wanted to get to know us well before placement. This gave us ample time to develop a beautiful relationship with them; one we continue to build together today. Then, our third and most recent adoption was a full two-year process. As an orphan in a foreign country, we knew of her, but we were not certain she would be ours until a few long weeks before returning home with her. However, with each adoption road traveled, we experienced even greater levels of joy and even more life-altering challenges. In some cases, the waiting time for a journey to end—or even begin! —may be shorter than other times. Regardless of the length of time, we are learning to try to discover the beauty that can be found *in* the waiting. Finding joy in the journey is the point I'm trying to make.

Have you embraced the idea that it takes patience throughout an entire adoption experience? You need patience during the process, patience with paperwork, patience with the loss of control, and patience with God's plan. The clock ticks on, the leaves fall from the trees, and other families continue to grow while you feel left out in the dust if you have not learned the virtue of patience.

In similar fashion, an authentic and deep human connection doesn't happen overnight. It must build and grow over time. Anything that takes time takes patience. We live in an instant gratification world, but most things worth having do not offer quick results.

Early on in our marriage, my husband was a student at Utah State University, and I was working as a nurse. We attended a church where our congregation was primarily newlywed college students. There were constantly new couples moving in, new babies being born, and families were growing all around us. Along with the change in perspective I learned during our time there, I also learned many lessons about patience.

Each week at church, there would be a newly married couple announcing their first pregnancy, or another family welcoming baby number two, while I sat there with empty arms, waiting for my turn to carry a little bundle of joy and share my own trumpeted announcement. How do you embrace the virtue of patience when each day drags on slower than the day before? How do you allow patience in when yearning for what your heart desires? One way that I tried to have patience was to fondly name myself the "grandma" of the ward, being one of the oldest women of the congregation at 26 to 28 years old, as I also declared myself the official baby holder.

The sting of pain and longing was soothed through service toward other mothers. Being jokingly called a "grandma" helped lighten the frustration of not being a mother. I loved that title and to this day, I own it. I've become great at holding babies and am sometimes called a baby whisperer as I can calm a crying child, gently rocking them to sleep, almost every time. It was difficult to be patient in my pain, but knowing that I can serve another mother, disheveled from a long night of little to no sleep, still gives me pure satisfaction. Being in the service of another is an edifying way to help pass the time, by taking the focus off of oneself. It sure helped me learn to find more patience. While focusing on their needs, my own pains dissipated. I was no longer wallowing in my own needs; I was helping them in their needs. Being able to allow my thoughts envelope them, kept my thoughts away from my own agonizing wait. It made the time creep by a little faster, by getting my "baby fix", even if just for a moment of snuggles.

The process of building connections takes time, and time can be painful. Patience is learning to enjoy the journey along the way before reaching the destination. Most of us desire human connection in our relationships with others, whether it be friendships, companionship, or parenthood, and seizing the opportunities to learn about life that arise while enduring the wait and taking the time to learn about others and grow personally, gives you joy as you practice patience.

Early on, and throughout our infertility journey, I often found myself in a "wo is me" frame of mind. Why was this happening to me? Why was everyone else able to have children biologically and I couldn't? Why was I not able to embrace patience? In the thick of it all, you can feel so alone in your trials. I know now that I am not the only infertility warrior, but it certainly felt that way sometimes.

Why? Because I wasn't allowing myself to sit with patience in my own story. How can we be patient when we are experiencing our most difficult challenge? First, by recognizing we are not alone. Oh, how we are so not alone. There are many who suffer in their own stories. And guess what, many who relish in their own stories as well. Second, by knowing this story was written on purpose for us. Remember, God is the author and he doesn't make mistakes. And third, by wrapping your arms around patience and letting the story happen. When you fall short, do you brush your trial or frustration aside, or do you grab on and face the problem head on, to be able to overcome it? Regardless, remember to have patience and give yourself grace.

Why do we have to have patience though? In James 1:3-4 (KJV) we read,

"Knowing this, that the trying of your faith worketh patience. But let patience have her perfect work, that ye may be perfect and entire, wanting nothing."

We must be tried to become perfect in Christ, perfect in patience. Sometimes we have to sit with the pain, the trial, and natural occurrence of God's timing. We must allow patience her opportunity to work in us. If we don't, we cannot grow in faith and in the patience of our trials.

I believe the same to be true in our relationships with others. Allowing the time and having patience in that timing helps human connections grow stronger. Growth comes from struggle, and struggle is, by definition, hard. But there can be joy in the act of patience through our struggles. For example, when our daughter was just 15 months old and still learning to walk, it was truly a joy to see her make progress in each step, even as she struggled along with her chubby little legs.

I was getting my photography business off the ground at that time, and often made use of my husband and daughter as my models. One of our more memorable photo sessions was at a beautiful park in Colorado Springs. Our favorite picture came after we took a moment and spent time allowing Kya to practice walking. She walked toward her father, leaving the safety and stability she felt in my grasp. She is a cautious thinker, and we could see her contemplating the daring act she was about to commit. While almost within the reach of her dad's secure open arms, stretched out from his squatting tall frame, she lunged forward with scarcely enough power left in her tired legs to end her little journey. She had taken three big steps to get there. A successful attempt at walking. She then rested her head on her daddy's knee, exhausted and happy, mustering just enough energy to look into the camera with warmth and satisfaction, her patience and persistence had been rewarded. This was a time when the wait was most certainly worth it and being able to capture the whole thing on film made the moment all the sweeter.

In the previous chapter where I discuss perspective, I was sharing our story of waiting for our first daughter. There were many opportunities for us learn the value of patience. The time spent while completing the paperwork, patience was found in understanding the knowledge we were gaining in the education of how adoption works. Our waiting for each child from the time of approval or that "paper pregnancy", patience is found in the mental and physical preparation when expecting a baby to come into your home. I loved the planning and shopping and decorating that happened during this time. I decorated the nursery, or bedroom in the case of our last adoption where our daughter was 12 at the time, with pure joy. I loved painting and choosing colors for the bedding. Shopping for décor to hang on the walls that adorned each room. Patience in waiting. Even the time it took once we were "chosen" until baby or child came home. Patience, waiting without frustration, was found in the excitement of it all.

Patience in the human connection comes from seeing others as humans, imperfect and messy humans. Just as we all are ourselves. Only Jesus Christ was the only perfect human on earth.

And even He needed to learn patience in all his trials. Remember at the beginning of the chapter when patience was defined as waiting "without frustration". Things are said in a relationship, feelings can be hurt, differences arise, but when we are patient with the humanity of relationships, then a genuine connection can be made. Having patience and grace for that humanity is one sure fire way to allow for a connection.

CHAPTER 3

Op"E"n

"The moment you're ready to quit is usually the moment right before a miracle happens.... don't give up." – Author unknown

Giving up is so easy when things do not go the way we plan or want. It's easy for us to just brush our trials aside and say we're done with it. But can it be done as easily as that? Is it truly easy when it's concerning something which you cannot stop thinking about? Can you really give up on those things that weigh heavy on your mind and keep you awake at night because they are very important to you? Do you really want to let something hold you back from moving forward and becoming who you are meant to be and fulfilling all you are meant to do?

"Four more to go," I would encourage my clients on their last few reps while lunging across the gym floor. I could see the strain and fatigue in their eyes, could see it written clearly on their faces, and could visualize the fight in their minds. They would think of giving up and quitting before finishing the last two drops and I sometimes wondered if I should really make them finish since they've worked so hard and really put in a great effort. Surely two more reps wasn't going to make the difference. Or would it? Yes. Even though they may not have been the actual repetitions that would sculpt their quads and hamstrings, those last few reps would help them learn to push past the pain, to build the mental strength and will power to go further the next time, to carry on when the going really gets tough.

Even in small moments of success, miracles happen. Don't sell yourself short just before that happens.

Embrace

"Owning our story and loving ourselves through the process is the bravest thing we'll ever do." – Brene Brown

Being as open as we are with our adoptions is not only a building block for getting us through the difficult times, but also a God-given blessing. Sometimes I will hear people say they wish they had the courage to share more. There is a fear that sharing your story is too personal and sacred. And while there is some truth to that, how often have we felt buoyed up by other's stories? Have you ever felt power in your own story when you were able to share it with others, and in return offer valuable strength for another's story? There is also a time and a place for all things. A season if you will. In Ecclesiastes, chapter 3 verse 5 (KJV), we read, "...a time to embrace, and a time to refrain from embracing."

How many times have you heard another's story and thought to yourself how you could relate? How can we learn to embrace our own story from the example of others? The similarities in others' stories are sometimes too close for comfort. But this is how human connection is born. Our stories are not the same, but the insight gained from each road bump can be synonymous. Everyone is facing a mountain of emotions, trials, or just day to day stressors . . . EVERYONE. Therefore, having the courage to share is a way to reach out to others and say, "I understand," or to offer a little empathy for another. Helping others to embrace their own story is one way to create authentic human connections. It's powerful to own your story enough to in turn be a shoulder to cry on, a helping hand, and source of power for someone else.

Brene Brown said it this way in her book Gifts of imperfection, "It is in the process of embracing our imperfections that we find our truest gifts; courage, compassion and connection." Courage is when you embrace imperfection, the compassion to be kind to yourself and to others, and then also be able to have connection with others because of your authenticity.

When you truly embrace your story or own your power that grew from that story, you aren't fearful of what others will say about your journey or how you learned from it, because it is yours. You were stretched and molded from your journey. Nobody can experience it the same way you did, and nobody can take away from your story, because it was written just for you by a loving God above. Have the courage to own it, to embrace it. Whether you share it with the world, or carefully tuck it away into your soul and protect it for just you, that's you embracing your truth.

During our journey in infertility, time went on and I continued to press forward, not very gracefully, but I tried. The "waiting" is the worst and I don't do it well. But after so many "plans" had changed in my life, I tried to focus on having faith that my loving Heavenly Father had done a great job with the changes thus far, and therefore probably had a great plan for me, even when I didn't understand where my story was going.

Throughout our "paper pregnancy" we were taking classes and meeting others who were facing similar trials on their own adoption journeys. It was comforting to have this support system. Even with family and friends who loved us and were there for us . . . it was just different to have support from others who really understood what we were feeling and dealing with. I heard others' stories and experiences and loved that. I heard stories that were just perfect for them and seemed so "planned" for them. I began to pray, often, that if I was to be a mother, that I would just "know" when it was my turn. I prayed that our story would be unique to me, to us, for us. "If I couldn't have MY PLAN, then please let Your plan be special for me," were my prayers.

After meeting the first birthmother we talked to, and feeling such an empty feeling, we began to pray, A LOT. How could I turn away a child when I wanted one so bad? How could this not be my child? Wasn't it my turn? Was this a cruel joke just to torture me? How could God get my hopes up and then tell me, nope, this is not your birthmother or child. I prayed hard, wore holes in my jeans at the knees. I prayed that if this was not our child, please send ours soon. I couldn't handle the disappointment of turning down this child yet, even though I knew this child wasn't ours. After much thought, Carl and I decided to move forward, slowly, with this birthmother. We would continue to communicate with her and support her in her journey. We would embrace this chapter of our story with open arms for this birth mother, not entirely sure where our story would lead us. Hoping this was God's plan for us and praying with faith.

The very next Friday after meeting the first birth mother, we got "The Call" from Jerica. She was due in a week. WOW. Was this for real? Carl called me and said, "this feels right, she sounds amazing." There wasn't much time, considering her due date, so we dropped everything and drove to meet her and her family. Their home was warm, welcoming, and there was a comfortable feeling surrounding us. We sat on the couch opposite the other couch, where her parents sat. One by one, her siblings walked in the room to join us. There are only a few things I remember about that conversation, but I distinctly remember feeling like family, and yet kind of like we were in a job interview, the most important job we will ever have.

There were many emotions and much internal dialogue taking place as we got to know one another. I remember Jerica's parents being concerned that we might be bothered if the baby was short, when we are so tall (Carl is 6'5" and I am 5'9"), and the baby's family members were much shorter. My concern was "are we good enough to be the parents of her baby?".

Jerica was so young, and so beautiful inside and out. You could see that in her demeanor right away. I kept trying to imagine what her baby would look like. I felt love for her in an instant, I not only wanted to have her love us, I wanted her to know that we loved her. She needed to know that we unconditionally loved her for the young woman she was and that we appreciated the loving choice she was making for her child. We wanted to know all about her as a person. It was hard to sit there and worry that she might think we just wanted the baby and didn't really care about her or her family. That couldn't be farther from the truth. No birthmother was ever or will ever be an "incubator" for us. They are so much more. They are my sisters now, they are family, they are imperfectly amazing women, then and now.

I remember talking with Carl early on in our marriage about the children we would have, like we all do when we get married and plan for a family. We would start with two boys, who would grow up to be taller than their mama and protect me as an old woman. Then we would add in a girl to bring in some softness and balance to our home—a little girl whose older brothers would dote over her and protect her on the playground at school. This was Carl's ideal family; I still wanted the 17 children I had dreamt of.

While we spoke with Jerica and her family, I remember wondering, "Was this really His plan for us? For me? Had our unique story begun?" Jerica lovingly held her stomach and announced that they'd just found out the sex of the baby and it was a little girl. I was so excited, none of those dreams of having a boy first mattered anymore. I didn't care. All I could imagine was being a mother. That was when Jerica's mother mentioned that the baby was "grown in Hawaii." In that exact moment, I had such a strong feeling that this was our baby. This was when I completely embraced our story, when I fully embraced how our story was unfolding. Since I was born in Hawaii, I felt as though that was God's way of telling me, this baby was to come to our home, we would get to raise this little girl. I wholeheartedly was embracing the story God was writing for us. The evening ended with such a warm and cozy feeling; I didn't want to leave their home. I wanted them to feel as comfortable as I felt.

I was trying to embrace these moments of meeting birth moms and being present in the part of the journey we were in. Embracing the moments with them and allowing for human connections to be created. Each one of them came with unique and beautiful souls. Some of the most important attributes to acquire for authentic connections are to first embrace who you are right now and then to embrace who others are. Unconditionally. We simply cannot make profound connections if we do not embrace our stories genuinely. Throughout my infertility journey there were many times I fought my truth. Why can't I have children biologically? Why did this have to be my story? It wasn't until I learned to embrace my story and love it, accepting the painful parts that I was able to give more of myself to those connections.

In adoption, embracing your part needs to be handled with extreme care, but you can still be fully integrated into the story. When our first child was about to be born, it was important for me to communicate my feelings about being in the delivery. I wanted to be there, not only for Jerica as her support, but to also ensure I was there to enjoy this step. Had I not played a part by expressing that, I may have missed out on a very beautiful experience. Jerica invited us to be there in the delivery room for this momentous and sacred occasion. A gesture I will never take for granted and will always be grateful for. Later on, we were also invited to be in our son's delivery. Another gesture of kindness I will forever be grateful from from Tess (our son's birthmom). I believe this to be one of the most significant actions we took toward forging our open adoption connections.

Excited to be part of the experience, as soon as they scheduled her to be induced, we made the drive. It was all such a blur. I remember talking with Carl about names. I have always loved this part of the journey. Naming a baby is a serious thing; heaven forbid you name them something that will cause them childhood torture on the playground. The name had to be special. It had to mean something. We tossed around quite a few names, each offering a choice and the other either considering or refusing the name. We even considered names that I had written down in my 'book of dreams.' This was a book of all the things I had dreamt of for my future as a teenage girl. Remember, I knew I was going to have seventeen children, and I had been prepared with a name for each one. However, the situation this time was different. This baby was being given to me by another, so the choosing of the name was extra important.

When we had met with the first birthmother, before Jerica, and had thought we might be the parents of twin girls, we had thought Zoe would be a good name, as I have always loved the name. And Carl came across the name Kia, from the car. But he suggested we change the spelling to K Y A. Zoe and Kya . . . yup that fit well for twin girls. Of course, it was not twins this time. With this baby, we thought, "why not give her my middle name?" After all, I was born in Hawaii, and she was "grown in Hawaii."

You see, when I was born, my parents had picked out the name Ginger Ashley. Not a bad name, but it certainly didn't fit me when I was born. So, my dad went to some of the Hawaiian women he knew from church, asking for Hawaiian names. He picked the name Kanani. He was also advised to name me after himself (I was daughter number four, and they'd already giving one of my sisters my mother's name). Thus, I became Paula (after Paul) Kanani. Kya Kanani. The name rolled off my tongue. It was perfect. I couldn't wait to share our thoughts with Jerica. We had discussed baby names with Jerica previously and we wanted to hear her choices now that the baby was on her way. When we arrived at the birthing center, she asked us what name we chose, and said that all she wanted was for her to have a Hawaiian name. Done! She too fell in love with the name Kya Kanani. We also asked Jeff (her birth father) what he would have wanted. He came up with a great name, suggesting that we name her after his mother. However, Kya Kanani just seemed so right, and he soon agreed with the choice.

Being with Jerica for her labor and delivery was a long, yet fun experience, for me. Not sure Jerica will share in my feelings of fun, but she was a warrior in her own story for sure. We passed the time watching movies, painting her toe nails, rubbing her feet, and doing whatever we could for her. I was so grateful to be able to pamper her during a time of need and difficulty. I wanted to be there for her and comfort her. Beyond the fact that we would soon be parents to her baby, it was important for me to play a part in her happiness. Being able to participate in this moment was one of the greatest gifts Jerica could give to us, aside from giving us parenthood and placing her child with us of course. Her parents were there, as well, and it was a great time to really get to know them better. Poor Jerica was progressing slowly and struggling with all that was going on. While walking down the hall to help move things along, she stopped for a rest and said behind gentle tears, "Can't I just go home and wait to turn seventeen to have a baby?" It was only four days away from her seventeenth birthday.

Labor was getting difficult and she started to feel the pain. I watched as they poked and prodded her innocent youthful body. I held her hand as she squeezed mine and her mother's on the other side of the bed while she winced with labor pains. It was suggested that she get an epidural. I haven't experienced this particular pain, and even if I had wanted to have a "natural" birth for myself, I prayed she would choose to go through this with the least amount of physical pain as possible. Didn't she have enough to deal with, emotionally? She chose an epidural.

She was so cute once the epidural kicked in, poking at her legs, giggling about how she couldn't feel them. We had a good laugh with that one. The day turned into night. All of us were tired, and the nursing staff was so great to set me up in a room next to Jerica's. Carl left to get some sleep and I rested on my hospital bed for a bit before I was awakened by some commotion. Approximately 15 or so hours after inducing Jerica, things were starting to happen.

Kya Kanani was born at 6:37 am on August 2nd, 2006. What a glorious day. She was beautiful, as are her birthmother and birthfather. She was perfect and healthy, ten fingers, ten toes. The doctor wrapped her up and took her to the baby warmer, where he checked her over and then said, "Who gets her first?" I was exploding inside: ME ME ME. Could I say that and be selfish and grab her in my arms? No. It wasn't my place to be selfish with her; it still isn't. I was completely committed to making this day be as easy as possible for Jerica, so I kept my mouth shut and waited. Grandpa (Jerica's father) got to hold Kya first. He held her for a few moments, then choking back tears, he handed her to me. I couldn't believe the emotional wave that poured over all of us. The love in that room at that moment was thick. You could feel it and see it; it was real. I was so grateful to be a part of the delivery and experience that with Jerica and her parents. It was also so surreal to watch the physical pain on her face from labor and delivery, knowing there was a deeper emotional pain she was carrying. My best day was her worst. How was that fair? The fairness only comes when considering the human connections being created from this part of the story. From the empathy and love we felt for her selfless act of love and hopefully the love she felt from us offered her the opportunity to embrace us. Her story is much different than ours, however being able to embrace each other's stories and allow for the connections to be made is what makes our open adoption journey work.

This baby was instantly loved by so many people. It was evident in the next couple days at the hospital. I am not sure if Kya kept any food down the day of her birth, I believe being held by so many people just didn't offer this tiny body to digest food properly. My older sister had recently had a baby of her own and was weening him off of breastmilk. She so generously donated some of her milk to me for Kya, however I honestly think she didn't keep most of it down. Poor girl. It was a busy day with many visitors. Kya was cuddled and held and loved by so many family and friends. Many came to meet this little girl thinking they would never see her again. This was their chance to meet her, whisper in her ear how loved she was, and then say goodbye. Strangers (us) were going to take her and raise her.

We had a family photo session at the birthing center that Grandma (Jerica's mother) arranged to have done. To this day, I am so grateful for those pictures. I dressed Kya in a beautiful dress and handed her to someone to hold, while a cousin of Jerica's, just six years old at the time, came up and sat next to me and said, "Is Jerica giving you her baby?" "Yes," I said. "That is really nice of her to do." Why yes, little one, that is the most precious gift anyone could ever give; life and love to your child, and on top of that, parents to raise her. I bawled my eyes out, again. I didn't run dry of tears, although you would think I would have with all the crying going on. The unity that was felt in that birthing center was more than I could understand. How could so many people feel like family, so quickly? My parents came to visit. Carl's parents came to visit. Jeff and Jerica's families and friends were there. Is this what family is all about? It is what I believe family to be, even more now than I did then. This was a great story and I wanted to be sure to be a part of it. I was learning to own every bit of that day that I could. Soak it all in.

I was learning to see how making valuable human connections was important for our story. Patience was needed as I knew this little baby girl needed rest, but I also wanted to share her with the world. There were so many people that day, and I didn't know most of them. I was beginning to see how I could connect with all of them and obtain a human connection even for a moment. The simple connection is this case, a tiny little baby girl that we all loved. I was optimistic about her future, knowing that she could learn to make her own connections with people from the example of love shown to her. Being able to embrace the story in each tender moment seemed vital to these connections, embracing everyone else's story and perspective of how this open adoption could work. Human connections are made in many ways and with many different stories. This day was an important part of our story in how we have learned to make authentic human connections.

Two days after Kya's birth, papers were signed and gifts exchanged, and many loving hugs and tears of sadness and joy were had. Jerica dressed Kya in her outfit to go home. I loved watching her dress her. I know that wasn't easy to do knowing she was about to hand over this little angel to another mother. It's a relationship like no other, two mothers loving one child, both with so many hopes and dreams for this little one. We embraced each other in that moment. We embraced the moments we had together as this little girl's mothers. We embraced the journey we were each about to take, separately. I embraced her story about to unfold, going home with empty arms and knowing full well that this would not be easy for her. I was trying to embrace how she would feel, but only with love and empathy could I embrace that. She was embracing the fact that I would be raising her child and loving her unconditionally, endlessly.

We bundled Kya in her car seat and walked out the front door one way, while Jerica and her parents turned the other way to go to their home. What an odd feeling. I didn't want to say goodbye to Jerica in that moment. I wanted us all to go home and love on this baby. I wanted to have Jerica by my side as I embraced this. However, I knew that would have been difficult for her and therefore, it was good to walk away for the moment. Home was also still a couple of weeks away as we were required to stay in Idaho state lines until given permission to leave. This is how adoption works. You cannot take the baby across state borders without clearance from both states.

There's an unspoken emotion that you feel when you walk away from a placement. I was thrilled to start being a mother, something I dreamt about for years. I was overjoyed and bursting at the seams from excitement of this new chapter. In the same breath, you feel extreme heartache for the instant family you have just gained. They are family, and it wasn't fair to walk away with something so precious to them. My emotions were split, and my heart was being torn in two. I deeply wanted to stay with her and have us share in each joyful moment together. I wanted to work on my relationship with Jerica and see that connection thrive. However, it just couldn't happen that way. We had to have that initial separation and practice patience so we could authentically build our relationship for the future. Being willing to embrace our stories and draw support from the experiences of others has led to what we have today and the openness we get to share now.

As a family photographer, I spend a lot of my time adjusting my lens to focus on the subjects in my view. If I don't dial in and embrace where the lens has to be for focus to happen, my clients won't be happy with the end result. If I don't adjust my focus properly and produce clear images, they can't share their story clearly. There then becomes an obvious disconnect. Similarly, if I don't take the time to embrace the adjustments needed for a clear view of my own story or who I am, how can I offer anything of value to others for that connection? The connection between us becomes out of focus. Look inside and adjust your focus, embrace your divine nature as you are now so you can give clearly to others. Then in return you can embrace their story and a connection is created.

I look at the three children we have now, the seven sets of very involved grandparents, the four biological parents and the handful of caregivers from an orphanage home we have created deep connections with, and I see my story in a way I can embrace whole heartedly. I wouldn't change any of our story. Why? Because it was written just for me, for us. With this perspective, I can embrace my story, and others, with open arms, making authentic human connections.

<u>Empathy</u>

"Your job is not to judge. Your job is not to figure out if someone deserves something. Your job is to lift the fallen, to restore the broken, and to heal the hurting."
– author unknown

Everyone deserves love and it is our job to provide it. We are to present ourselves as instruments in God's hands in service to all His children. Everyone will fall, everyone will hurt, and everyone will be broken for moments of time. Who are we to even consider anything but empathy and love as we hoist each other up when it is needed the most? A dear friend of mine from my youth fought a fierce battle of cancer, and among all her difficult days she continued to smile. She once told me, "Smile, it makes people wonder what you are thinking." You can be the light for another in a smile as she was for me. Empathy aids you in understanding how to bring light in for others.

In Matthew 5: 14-16 (KJV) we are taught, "Ye are the light of the world . . . let your light so shine before men." That light within us comes from God and our Savior, Jesus Christ. This is where we find the strength to lift others, to help restore them when they are broken and to heal their pain—through empathy for their story. We are God's tools in service; we have been given talents to do such service.

My oldest daughter has never been much of the 'girly' type. She never played with dolls. Animals have always been her choice of companion throughout her childhood. She didn't care to try on lipstick, dig into my makeup bag, or walk around in my red heels. She did however jump into her dad's hunting boots and threw on a cowgirl hat a time or two . . . or a hundred. She dances to the beat of her own drum. I admire her for her courage to be unique. It is something I pray she will always possess. I fondly remember one of those times she tried on those boots and staggered throughout the house with careful and methodical steps. She has always been a very cautious achiever. I watched her and wondered why kids enjoy stumbling around in shoes ten times their size. Is it because they are pretending to be just like mom or dad? Possibly. Or is it simply an attempt to grow up? I didn't like that idea; they grow up a little too fast already.

What if we were to put a twist on that perspective and imagine that they were learning what empathy is. Perhaps they are asking "What it is like to walk in another's shoes? What it is like to be charitable? What it is like to experience their trials, hardships, and the joys of their journey?" Did my daughter see how she could literally feel the worn and molded soles or the soul inside of her father's journey by walking in his boots? Did she understand where he had walked to get to be her father? Could we in return do the same for others? What about our birth families? Could we foster a greater sense of compassion and empathy for the road they had to travel to bring them to the decision to place their precious children into our arms? In adoption, open or closed, empathy and compassion are vital for a successful experience. The Dalai Lama said this about empathy, "Love and compassion are necessities. They are not luxuries. Without them, humanity cannot survive." (*The Art of Happiness*) Empathy is compassion. Empathy is charity. When expressed honestly and deeply, our love for our children, no matter how they come to us, is so much greater than can be expressed. And in turn, we can have a greater love for those who brought them to us.

As a college student, I worked as a nurse's aide in an assisted living facility. Daily, I had the privilege of assisting some of my sweet residents to the dining room for dinner. Their pace was always slow, and they sometimes staggered or stumbled as they shuffled from place to place. As we walked arm in arm, we would talk, and they would share their life stories with me. I imagined what I would have done had I gone through some of the fascinating life experiences many of them had gone through. As they struggled to walk, their feet shuffling along the floor, I wanted to carry them, to ease their weary bodies and place them in their seats at the table with compassion. I truly desired to see their burdens lightened. And to be the one to lighten it for them. I wanted to gain a genuine understanding of them, then help to carry their load.

Within the adoption experience, empathy can come when we desire to lift our birth families' spirits. Charity comes when we put aside all judgments and love unconditionally. When we unconditionally love them for who they are and how our lives are connected, but with a clear understanding that we cannot change the outcome of the hardships. Why does my loss of fertility bring me to be so deeply connected to the choice of another to gift parenthood over their own right to parent? How and why are lives connected in this way may not always be something we need to understand. We face trials to help us grow, and we can grow together in adoption. When we have experienced any loss, sorrow, or pain in a similar way to another person, we can feel empathy for them. Empathy is "Seeing with the eyes of another; listening with the ears of another; and feeling with the heart of another." (Attributed to Alfred Adler) Having regard for another's feelings or circumstances.

I was sitting on a plane, on a flight to San Diego, next to my husband and surrounded by our friends. Excitement filled the cabin as our official 'new chapter' was about to begin. My husband and I were blessed to be a part of a non-profit organization. We were expanding the charity from small town Idaho to five new states, and still growing. Carl likes the window seat, which allows for me to snuggle right up to his shoulder and look out at the blanket of clouds hovering outside. During this flight, I was enchanted with the glorious light from the sun as it danced on top of the clouds. I was lost in my thoughts and embraced the peaceful and bright view. That is, just until moments later when the plane began to descend, falling slowly below the clouds, where gloomy gray skies greeted us. How strange for something so beautiful to go from bright warmth to a bleak chill so quickly. But the light was still there. It was all about my perspective. Often when we truly understand how empathy resonates in our hearts, we can see past the gloom. We see above the clouds and up to the glorious glow that God offers us daily.

God will stand with you when you draw close to Him and give it all to Him. With human strength we can do nothing alone, but He gives abundant strength when we draw near. When we ask,

He gives, when we seek, He shows us the answers, and when we knock, He answers and opens the doors wide open for us to enter.

If, with empathy, we have "regard" for another's circumstances, how can that translate to someone's experiences within adoption? I have never been pregnant, so naturally I have not given birth. Therefore, I often think about how I can have empathy for a birth mom who has. Can I have empathy for birth parents who choose adoption for their children? I believe yes. I have not experienced their experiences, but I have a high regard for their circumstances. I recognize and acknowledge the heaviness of their journey. I respect their stories for what they are. Empathy can come as we seek to understand each other, and as we learn each other's stories. This is Jerica's story:

"Let me introduce myself: My name is Molly. Actually, it is Jerica, but Molly was a nickname I received my freshman year of high school. It is short for "Molly Mormon." I was the epitome of Molly Mormon. I didn't drink caffeinated drinks, I didn't watch PG-13 movies, I had never said a swear word in my life (and if you swore around me, I would let you know that I didn't appreciate it). So yes, I was a little bit extreme. Which, I was proud of! I was proud that people knew my standards. My clothing was very modest; not tight, high neck, shorts to my knees. I read and prayed daily, went to church weekly, and attended a bible study class called seminary. I had never drunk or done drugs, and because people knew how firm I was about my religion, they never offered them to me. I had plenty of friends who all shared my same values. I didn't care about being the most popular or the hottest girl in school. I was content with living my life the way it was.

Then I met a boy.

He was new in school, and he was "hot!" He played football, he was buff, he was nice and he was one of the "popular guys." It didn't take him long to get a girlfriend. He dated the really pretty girls who were also "popular." I never, in a million years, thought he would go for me. So, I didn't go out of my way to get his attention. I just admired from a distance.

I was only fourteen at the time when we became desk mates in a class. Not only was I attracted to him, but I also quickly found out that he was attracted to me. We soon became boyfriend and girlfriend.

I began to change who I was for him. I started keeping things from my parents, like "dating" this boy before turning sixteen. I started to drink caffeinated drinks and going to R-rated movies with him. I even lost all my good friends because they didn't like the way I was behaving. This went on for nearly two years. When I finally turned sixteen, he took me on an official date. My parents didn't know we had already been exclusive for so long, so they thought this was my first date with him. We were in love, so we thought.

Soon after our first official date he started dating another girl and I was left behind. I was devastated. I wanted to be with him. I didn't have any of my old friends, and my new friends didn't hang out with me because they were his friends. It was a heartbreaking situation for me. Just a few weeks had gone by, which felt like forever, until I found out that I was pregnant. What was I supposed to do? Everyone would know very soon what I had done. How my changed behaviors had caused me to do things that should have been saved for marriage. They would know. My parents would know. This thought was agonizing. Silver lining: maybe he would want to be with me and our baby, and even marry me.

After telling my brother and going to the crisis center to confirm the pregnancy, they gave me three options. 1. Keep the baby. 2. Adoption. 3. Abortion. What was I going to do?

Many months, prayers, and decisions later, I decided on adoption. Then the realization of needing to choose a family to raise my child settled in. I didn't know where to begin but found an agency through my church to help.

We know what she decided. She placed her beautiful baby girl into my arms as her new mother. While my story is not the same as Jerica's, my empathy for her grew in knowing her story. My regard for her circumstances is deep in my heart. It is because of this level of empathy that our relationship is what it is today. Later I will share our son's birthmother's story, in Tess's own words. Knowing her story gave me the same opportunity to build empathy and understanding as we developed our relationship and formed a deep, authentic human connection.

Our open adoption story began right away with our first child. The level of openness in such relationships is going be different for everyone, and assuming the best interest of the child is everyone's number one priority, open adoption can mean anything. For us, we felt that if our children remember the day, we told them they were adopted, we waited too long. We wanted our children to know who they are, where they came from, and to embrace that about themselves. We speak often, and candidly, in our home of the traits we see in our kids that come from their birth families. We play the "nature vs. nurture" game and talk about who gets credit for different personality traits. Since we know our birth families so well, it's easy to pick out who claims what. Our "nature vs nurture" game has become an act of endearment in our home. "Oh, that bit of sassiness must be from Mom, and her calm, cautious ways must be from her birth mom."

To this day, we still enjoy seeing all the talents and amazing traits in our children shine through, and we love that we know who those talents came from. It's in our nature as human beings to seek these connections. Having regard and empathy for the unique character traits we all have can serve us well as we shape our relationships with those around us.

Encompass

"I think it's very human, the hope that an all-encompassing love will change us into someone else, someone better."
– Jennifer Finney Boylan

We were quite spoiled with Kya; she was not your typical baby. She never had a "blow out" diaper, she didn't spit up much, and she started sleeping through the night by three weeks old. She was content just hanging out and she entertained herself. She didn't cry much at all nor was she very mischievous. Parenting 101, we could write the book on it. We sure knew what we were doing! (Can you hear the heavy sarcasm in my voice?) However, we have certainly been blessed with the children God placed in our homes and hearts. They say adopted children are little angels . . . well they are, and Kya proved that over and over to us. In fact, all our children have proved the statement to be true. Of course, we still have our fair share of parenting challenges, where each child has had us second guessing and questioning our abilities.

Not only were we learning to be all-encompassing in our relationships with our birth families, but we were evolving as parents in the basic human connections created with our children. Bonding came at different times with each child. There wasn't a nine-month natural bond. Therefore, some of our greatest human connections came within the walls of our own home as parents as we grew in the process. Parenting and the human connection have a lot in common. Even when you birth your children and the natural bond is formed, there still is patience, perspective, perseverance, embracing, an encompassing love and optimism that need to occur. These are just building blocks for authentic human connections.

When Kya was just four days old, we made a short trip back to the birthing center to do some blood work for her. Since it was also Jerica's birthday, we asked if we could stop by for a visit. So early in the relationship, we were a little uncertain of how we would be welcomed. What an amazing occasion it was to go back and spend more time with them, and to allow this little blessing in our arms to be the tie that bound us as families. Can a child really be loved by too many people? I'd say a loud and resounding, NO.

However, our openness and newly extended family wasn't as easy for everyone. I grew up in a home with six siblings and a stay-at-home mom. She is a great one, too. Her life was dedicated to her family and children. Everything she did was for us, and that was a blessing in my life, as well as for my sisters and brother. But as we got older and started to leave the nest, it wasn't easy for my mother. She wanted to keep us all to herself. What dedicated mother wouldn't want that? When my oldest sister got married, my mom, jokingly, but a little teary-eyed, told my new brother-in-law that she hated him for taking her daughter away. It is a great laugh for us all now, but it was not easy for her to share her daughter with someone else. As each child got married, she still felt the same. It became an unspoken wish for each of our spouses to get to hear the term of endearment, "I hate you," from Mom because we knew that meant we were so loved that she didn't want to share us.

Well, what do you do when you not only have to share your child with a spouse's family, but now you must share your grandchildren with several more sets of grandparents? This was not easy for my parents, or Carl's parents, at first. Which grandma gets time with their grandchildren this time? But what a wonderful problem to have! Isn't it great that so many people want to love a child?

We brag about the fact that our children have seven sets of grandparents . . . not including all the greats we have. We have a baker grandma with all sorts of goodies, we have a potato grandma with the cats and bunnies, we have a Hawaii grandma, we have a crafty grandma, we have our Abuela, we have a candy grandma, and we have the grandma with chickens for us to play with. All of them are great at giving the kids treats (behind Mom's back of course). "What happens at Grandma's, stays at Grandma's." We take this saying quite literally. Of course, we don't ever forget our wonderful grandpas, either! Within all this love from grandparents, our children are creating human connections as well. What a joy it is to watch as our children develop the traits necessary for genuine human connections, naturally. It's like second nature to them. They each come with their own God-given talents and attributes that strengthen those relationships. We do our best as parents to foster those talents and allow for the connections to be made.

During our pre-parenting daydreaming days, while imagining all the grand things we would do as parents—remember we thought we were experts in the field of parenting—it was very important to us to raise our children in a home where they would be taught to "love all people." Loving all people comes with a fair amount of all-encompassing love necessary. This is unconditional love, and kids are great at that. They do well to not bring in judgements and pre-conceived notions to the relationship. So, in a sense they were teaching us about how to "love all people", how to be all-encompassing. To love another human being is to accept their story unconditionally. To encompass love for others is to accept them just as they are and then build on that for a relationship to ensue.

As mentioned earlier, I grew up in a military family. We moved just about every two years to many different states and a few countries as well. I grew up meeting a lot of different types of people from different races, religions, ethnicities, circumstances, and stories. What I learned was that we are all God's children. I wanted my children to share my "love for all people." I have found that as our relationships with our birth families grew this love for all people began to become a natural thing for us. As unnatural as adoption may seem, it became natural for us to see others in an empathetic light. Within the world of adoption, purely by choices made, there must be an unconditional understanding or relationships won't last. Adoption is created for the sole purpose of providing a family for another's child. A choice is made by one that results in pregnancy, the following choice as hard as it is, is then adoption. Placing your child with a family, most often, strangers at first is a daunting decision. It doesn't come lightly. Life altering. If you cannot have an attitude of "loving all people" in adoption, the human connections simply will not form. Loving all people, especially for the choices made is pure charity and is all-encompassing.

In February 2007, our special weekend with Kya, just 6 months old, had arrived. Months of preparation, adoption case worker visits (*to ensure we really were competent parents*), sewing white dresses, pictures galore, invitations made and sent—everything was complete and ready. We were going to make this baby legally ours. Adoption finalization day came. We dressed in our best and Kya was just the cutest little girl I had ever seen. We drove to the courthouse, where we were met by my in-laws and Kya's birth mother and her parents. It was great to hear the judge deem us worthy parents. We were now legally "Mom and Dad." I was worried that this would be a difficult day for Jerica, but she was amazing. Gratitude radiated from her demeanor, and I loved that about her. How could she be so strong? I was so grateful to be able to share this day with her. I wanted her to see how much we loved her little girl. I wanted her to know that, through thick and thin, Kya would be loved and cared for. A couple days later, we were blessed to take Kya to the temple with us, to be sealed in our forever family.

I woke up on the morning of the 10th of February with as much excitement as I'd felt the morning of my wedding day. Our white clothes were clean and hanging, ready for the day. The air outside was a cool crisp blanket, and it was a glorious day. We packed up and headed to the Logan, Utah Temple. When we arrived, we met with some family before heading inside. I handed Kya off to a dear friend of ours, who was one of the temple workers. She got to care for Kya until it was time for the ceremony. I remember sitting there in the temple, looking around the room at all our family who were in attendance. All the seats were full and there were even guests standing behind those seated.

We were blessed to have my grandfather perform the ceremony, the same man who married/sealed Carl and me together in the same temple. It was very special. He began to speak to us and offer guidance for us as parents. He then said, "I feel impressed to say that we should have a love for all people." I lost it, bawling my eyes out. Wasn't this what I had dreamt for my children to learn, what I had prayed for my family to know? I looked around the room again and saw my parents, Carl's parents, our siblings, Kya's birth grandparents from both birth mom and birth dad, birth mom's brother, and some of our very close friends. Who were all these people? Family. That is all I could think of, these were my family. There is a song that is near and dear to my heart that includes the words, "It's love that makes a family." Was this not true in this moment, on this day? We were all family to this little Kya. Everyone in that room loved her and we all loved each other. It was encompassing love and you could feel it. Encompassing love because of one little human, she was creating the connection for all of us.

The next day, Carl, now legally Kya's father, blessed her. He blessed her with so many wonderful blessings—it was a beautiful father's blessing. We shared this day with those in the temple plus so many more family and friends. Jeff (Kya's birthfather), his dad and stepmom, and his mom and stepdad were there. Jerica and her brother sang a loving rendition of "Walk Tall You're a Daughter." My heart was overflowing with gratitude and love. Is this what loving ALL people meant? Encompassing love, bringing all the love and talents together to celebrate such an occasion is yet another crucial quality in forming human connections.

Birthdays came and family came with it. We moved and family was there. There was struggle and family was there for us. Mistakes were made and family still loved us. Family grew and we were welcomed. The point is family is what you make it.

Encompassing love has to be a component in the equation of human connections. Judgements need to be set aside when encompassing another into your relationships. Sure, we all make mistakes and sure nobody is perfect, but all too often we use our judgements of those imperfections as barriers to creating an authentic connection.

CHAPTER 4

Ope"N"

"I can't change the direction of the wind, but I can adjust my sails to always reach my destination."
– attributed to Jimmy Dean

As a young girl, I thought it would be fun to be a pirate captain. I would study my course. Ready the ship. I would spread out my maps and, with a compass in hand, the course to my destination would be charted. I would always strive to know where I was going and the best route to get there. Coupled with that, I would know the stops along the way and how long each stop would take. This is how a good captain runs her ship. But ofttimes, we are not the captains of our own ship and since the course is rough, the wind can blow our ship off course. When we feel like we've lost control of a situation, it often sends us into a whirlwind of emotions. We feel as Alice did while tumbling down the rabbit hole into Wonderland. It is sometimes difficult to find our bearings or even know where to plant our feet. But just one pause in the movement can offer a moment of calm; take this moment to adjust your sails and realize that the new course which God has placed you on is, most likely, far better than the fantastic course which you originally planned. Even the best intentions and the most beautiful plans may not necessarily result in great results. But God's way offers an opportunity for growth and learning. When you are on the new path which He has given you, embrace it and use what you already know to adjust your course: your new destination will be more beautiful than anything you can comprehend with your mortal mind.

Nourish

"Do not be dismayed by the brokenness of the world. All things break. And all things can be mended. Not with time, as they say, but with intention. So, go. Love intentionally, extravagantly, unconditionally. The broken world waits in darkness for the light that is you." – L.R. Knost

Feeling broken is normal. If we never break in some way or another, we have no way to grow or become stronger from our experiences. We may break physically, emotionally, or spiritually. Time helps broken people to mend, but it is the understanding that we need to be whole-hearted and live with intention that brings out a better light in each of us that can be used to fight back the darkness from which the world seems to be suffering. Relationships need to be carefully nourished and fed to thrive. Just as my pet gecko needed proper food nourishment to survive, so do relationships. Human connections need constant nourishment to withstand the trials of life, and trials within those connections. Nourishment doesn't need to take up all your energy, but consistent attention and focus is important. That is if you want to build a lasting and meaningful relationship. In order from my relationship with God to grow and be strengthened I must be praying consistently. Prayer is a form of communication with God. If a human connection needs communication, you talk, if it needs nourishment, you give it the care and attention necessary. Breathing life into a relationship may look like a simple text to tell someone you are thinking of them. A phone call, a gift, including others in your prayers. All these are ways to nourish the human connection.

And then there were four. Of course, it wasn't that easy, but it's a good start to the paragraph, right? We'd had our baby, Carl had graduated from grad school, and it was time to move on from college life. I wanted to move to the big city, and Carl is a small-town country boy, but we needed to find somewhere we both wanted to live. Before we had children, and shortly after Carl decided on a degree for his career, we had always talked about where we might want to live someday. The only place we could agree on was Colorado. So that always stuck with us. We'd focus our job hunt on Colorado. And Carl was offered a job in Colorado Springs, CO in the summer of 2007, the summer Kya turned 1.

We made the move to Colorado in October of 2007. We found a town house and began to set roots. In November of 2007, we started the adoption process again. We went through the whole nine yards for a second time—the paperwork, decisions, classes, and background checks. We were approved in March of 2008.

Around the same time, Carl was offered his old job back, in Idaho. We had explored options of opening a business in Idaho, and we hadn't heard from any birth moms at this point, so we decided to make the move back home near family. We were busy parents and had a lot of things going on, so the wait wasn't as bad this time around. But just because I was a mother didn't mean the sting of infertility was gone.

We left Colorado in June 2008. We often wondered why we were only in Colorado for only eight months, especially since our plans were to settle down and raise our family there. It became very clear to us just a few short weeks after our move.

The adoption process had changed a bit this time. Things were becoming more paperless than with our first adoption experience. While putting together our profile for our first adoption, I made a scrapbook page for birth mothers to get to know us better with actual paper in hand. This time, I started a blog for birth moms to go to and learn more about our family. It gave me an opportunity to update the content weekly, mostly with descriptions of our Friday Night Date/Family Nights. I started this blog while still living in Colorado, and our agency had access to the link for birth moms and dads to see. After moving back to Idaho and once we had settled in a bit, living in my parents' basement while we remodeled our first home, we transferred our adoption profile to the office in Idaho and then began to wait, again.

Everything was great. We had a home, a career, a new business in the works, and our little girl. We were patiently waiting for any news about another baby, but as we were so busy with so many changes, I had been neglecting my blog. It had been a month or so since my last post. One night, I was awakened by Kya for a midnight potty break. Once she was back in bed and sleeping soundly, I laid my head down and had the thought come to me, "It's been a while since I have updated the blog . . ." I was tired and groggy, but I just could not get back to sleep. I kept thinking "it's been a while since I updated the blog," over and over. Why couldn't I just go back to sleep? So, I got up and sat at my computer, and this is what I wrote . . .

"So, finally I am updating this blog. With all that has been going on lately I haven't been consistent with updating or even "Friday night family nights" for that matter. But we are still here and still praying for a sibling for Kya.

Honestly, its 3:00 a.m. and I was lying in bed, unable to go to sleep after our sweet little Kya woke up crying. I went in to calm her and take her potty and put her back to bed. After holding her for a few minutes, I said, "Mommy is going to go back to bed. "She replied with, "No, Mommy, hold Kya." So, I did. After a few more minutes, I laid her down, turned on her music, and went back to bed. Laying here thinking to myself, 'I need to update our blog,' and I felt I needed to do it now. So here I am, at 3:00 am, journaling some more of our latest activities."

This was on a Wednesday evening. The very next day, Thursday, the 24th of July, Carl, and I were working on the house and needed a break. We took off to grab a bite to eat for lunch. Let me paint a little picture for you: Carl and I were in our grubbiest, hats on head, no makeup (Carl was also without makeup) and just dirty, dirty, dirty, from paint and house remodel junk all over us. We were eating in a fast-food restaurant when my cell phone rang. Thoughtlessly, I picked it up. It was our caseworker saying there was a birthmother who had chosen us. Wait, what? How could this be? We hadn't even heard from any birth moms. Who had chosen us to be parents when we didn't even know who was looking at us? Who was she? Where was she from? When could we meet her? Was this for real? It was almost too good to be true.

We were being considered to be parents again. Both Carl and I began to cry, right there in the fast-food restaurant. We got some very interesting looks from others around us. Then we got an email a couple days later from Tess and Jon.

Tess and Jon, a young energetic couple looking for parents for their baby boy, introduced themselves with a picture and a descriptive email. Tess then told us she was having a difficult time choosing a family and had a few couples in mind. She shared with us that they had been following our blog and were disappointed that I hadn't updated for a while. Tess wanted to learn more about us and get to know us more, but I hadn't posted in a few months. She decided to pray and ask for some answers as to who her baby's parents should be. She prayed that we would post on our blog on a Wednesday. The same Wednesday night I wrote a blog post in the middle of the night.

She said her prayers were answered when she got onto the blog the next morning and I had posted . . . she knew in that very moment that she wanted us to be the parents for her child. Tess and Jon were only looking at profiles of families in Colorado. She learned about us before our profile had been transferred to Idaho. Hoping for an open adoption as well, she reached out to her case worker and told him she had chosen us. Open adoption was already our groove and adding more family to our family was an easy decision for us to agree to. Being able to nourish new relationships while grafting their family in to help strengthen our own was something we were more than willing to do.

She was only a few months pregnant when we were connected. She wanted to get to know the adoptive parents she would choose and develop a relationship with them well before the birth. We met Tess and Jon in person for the first time two months later when they came to Idaho and stayed with us for a weekend. We continued to nourish the relationship via frequent emails and calls. In December of 2008, I had the opportunity to fly to Denver to spend a weekend with them one last time before baby boy's due date. This was an amazing trip for me to connect with Tess. We became sisters at heart. While I was there, Tess had a doctor's appointment and she requested that they do an ultrasound so I could see baby boy for myself. Tears of joy rolled down my cheeks leaving salty lines on my face as I listened to this baby's heartbeat. By this time, we had already discussed names for him. He was named Zander.

Tess's main concern with the placement of her child was to ensure she knew her adoptive family well enough to feel comfortable with her decision. She wanted to build that connection early on in her pregnancy. She needed the relationship to have time to be nourished and thrive.

When you nourish something, you feed it for the purpose of growth, health, and good condition. This is exactly how we should approach the human connection: with open arms. To create a strong and healthy connection that will last, you must feed it properly. That is what this book has been about. What are we nourishing our relationships with? Hopefully, with a healthy perspective, along with patience and optimism for the future. Are we nourishing the growth of our relationships with optimism and love? We know that love is a huge factor for all good things: Are we approaching that love with an optimistic viewpoint, and with faith? Are we embracing each other and our circumstances, and having empathy for those circumstances?

As with all human connections, our open adoption relationships with both Jerica and Tess required a lot of nourishment. We were not able to connect face to face as easily with Tess due to our geographical distance. It took careful attention from all parties involved to develop and nourish the connection we have today. Open dialogue and purposeful communication were essential then and still are today.

Once adoption became our story, we created an "all-or-nothing" family circle. You want to be a part of the life of one of us, you get to have all of us. It's like when you marry your spouse—you also marry their family. Same goes here: get one, get all. We have appreciated so much how all our families have respected this and how all the grandparents love all of our children the same. It really is a beautiful thing to see. Every grandparent was excited about our news for baby number two. They all looked forward to welcoming this baby as much as they welcomed Kya to the family. They were ready to put in the effort to nourish this new relationship.

We were invited to be with Tess in the labor and delivery room: what a wonderful opportunity to nourish our relationship! Tess's due date was nearing, and I asked her to tell us when she got to four centimeters. "Call me and I will pack up and head to Denver," I said. It didn't matter to me if I had to wait a week. She had invited me to be at the birth, and I wasn't going to miss it. It was a twelve-hour drive, so we needed time to get there. She had a doctor's appointment a week before she was due and called me. To my surprise, she was not in full labor, but was already at four centimeters. This was Monday the 26th of January. I packed up, called my husband, and said, "I am leaving for Denver tonight. Are you able to come or should we fly you out later?" I wasn't going to miss a thing. After all, my new sister was about to have a baby, and this baby was joining our family. Carl decided he would come too and so we packed up the family, taking Kya with us, and left, arriving around 3:00 pm the afternoon of the 27th.

After some rest at home and a quick bite to eat, Tess and Jon met us at the hospital. The hospital staff checked on her and indeed,

Tess was in labor. After being admitted and settled into her room, it wasn't too long before she had an epidural started. No need to endure the physical pain when there were so many emotions to deal with. We had some great laughs along with some heartfelt tears in the labor and delivery room. Carl was there with me, as were Tess's mom and, of course, Jon.

Tess wanted some red popsicles to help make the time go by, but delivery wasn't too far away. Just a few short hours later, Tess was creeping up on nine centimeters and ready to push, suddenly there was a problem. Our strong-willed little boy wouldn't move his hand from his head, and therefore required an emergency cesarean delivery. They would only allow one person to go back in surgery with her. With a look of fear on her face, she looked at me, then asked that Jon go with her. It did not bother me at all; she was scared and needed someone familiar with her. I just wanted her to be calm and comfortable. It was important to me to be there for Tess emotionally. It's not about what we want when feeding a relationship. It's about focusing on other's needs and even wants. They wheeled her back to surgery and Carl, grandma L, and I waited patiently for the arrival of baby boy. The time seemed to go by quickly, and soon the nurse invited me into the recovery room to meet our son. Jon brought him out all bundled up. Zander was born in the very early hours of the 28th of January. It didn't take long for him to arrive; he was ready and anxious to get here. To this day, he is a busy boy and always on the go, much like his birth parents.

Jon handed Zander to me, and I fell in love. He had a wrinkly fore-head and tiny little features; he was perfect. The amazing staff of nurses set up a recovery room for me right next to Tess's room so we could share the nights with Zander. I asked the nurses to not take Zander to the nursery. If Tess needed some rest, then I'd like them to bring him in my room. I would care for him. I wanted to make sure he wasn't left alone and that, between his two mothers that night, he would be watched over and cared for.

The next day was busy with many phone calls to all our families, and every one of them was thrilled with the news. Our family was growing. Kya had a little brother and two more sets of grandparents.

We spent two weeks in Colorado before we got to return home to Idaho.

The next few months were again spent as new parents, adoring, and loving on our new baby boy. He definitely challenged us as parents. Zander is far more vocal than his sister and required a lot more hands on attention. Big sister wasn't sure how she felt about this new little crier in her home, but she went about her day as though the disruption wasn't there. Although they had two completely different personalities, they certainly looked like brother and sister. You wouldn't know these two little angels came from four different biological parents. They were meant to be brother and sister, just as we feel they were meant to be our children.

Before Zander's adoption finalization in court at six months old, we were visited by both sets of Colorado grandparents. These separate visits offered us the opportunity to share our children with them and nourish those relationships as well. Welcoming them into our family was easy, and we were welcomed into their families in return. The nature vs. nurture conversation often comes up with our families. Zander has so many amazing things about himself that resemble Tess and Jon. Even as a baby, we could see his birth parents in his soul. As an adoptive mom, I never see my children's personality traits and the nature of who they are without seeing their birth parents. Vocalizing these inherent traits, we see in our son became an important part of our connection to Tess and Jon. This is what they needed to be nourished with for our connection to strengthen and blossom.

One day, I realized that we needed to be nourishing our relationship with Tess more intentionally. Tess was saddened to hear us compare some of Zander's traits to us, his adoptive parents. It was unsettling for her to know that we saw some similar character traits and looked a bit like us. How was this possible? He came from her and Jon, not us. Without intentionally hurting her feelings, we had done just that. Soon after hearing of her concerns, we had a heart to heart discussion. Our relationship was needing more nourishment than it was getting. I told her, "Tess, there is not a day that goes by that I don't see you or Jon in our son. He has your eyes, and your outgoing personality. There will never be a day when I don't see you in him. Please know that there will always be a piece of you in him and I will see it and cherish it. But as his mother now, I also have to see the things in him that connect him to our family, too. It is important to raise him in our home where he will always feel loved and a part of us. I love you sis, and because I see you in him daily, I will do my best to raise him with as much love as I know you have for him."

As his mother, I needed to nourish that connection. Zander needed to grow up feeling like he fit in, or was truly a part of our family. I have always nourished that part of our relationship in many ways including telling him he and I have very similar personalities. As mentioned earlier, it is important to nourish the relationships within your own home to ensure proper growth for all. On the other hand, Tess needed to be nourished by hearing how her little boy was just like her. Her connection to him was important for her relationship with us as a family to develop and thrive. Nourishing that has been key to the survival and success of our relationship to this day.

Tess

When Paula first asked me to write this, I was a little shocked I hadn't already. And when I realized I hadn't, I decided to do some research on her blog to see the kind of things people wrote about, to see if I could give a different perspective. However, I learned I was overthinking much of it. So this is my story, Zander's birth mom, Tess Laeh.

I woke up around four in the morning in a panic. I had been so busy with school and working two jobs, it just occurred to me I was over a week late. Not too big of a deal; I'm usually irregular, right? But something in me felt different, as though I really didn't need to pee on that stick to know that I had really messed up. That I really didn't need that second little line to show up blue before I knew I was about to become a disappointment to my family, a laughing stock among my friends, and when it came right down to it, a really, really stupid girl. But lo and behold there it was, confirmation of everything that I was feeling showed up in the darkest blue that second line could possibly be - I was pregnant. How did I find myself in this predicament? Didn't I know the risks in what I had been doing? The answer was simple: I was in love, and I didn't care about anything other than that at the time. There were no consequences in my mind, I certainly wasn't thinking about another person's life who didn't even exist at the time, a person whose fate I held. I was nineteen, in love with a boy, and wanted to express it and be as close as possible to him. It was selfish, but try explaining that to my nineteen-year-old self. I called my boyfriend immediately, over and over again at four am, until he picked up. In a sleepy, panicked slumber I heard, "Is everything okay?" The only response I could muster was "No." "What's wrong, what's going on?" "I'm pregnant."

I don't remember the rest of the conversation at all. I knew this was way worse news for him than it was for me. After all, he was LDS (a member of the Church of Jesus Christ of Latter-Day Saints), his whole family was LDS, including all the siblings' significant others. I was already a monkey wrench, and now this. I felt awful. I knew how much the church meant to him, and how his family would react to learning he was sexually active before marriage, let alone getting a girl pregnant. Talks were had. We both morally hated the idea of abortion, and it wasn't even an option in either of our minds. The only other two choices were keep the child, or place the baby for adoption. We found out early enough that we could hide it from our families for a few weeks while we thought about what to do. I remember one big conversation we had. We were sitting at a park inside a car for hours. We both weren't ready for a kid, but we loved each other and thought maybe the responsible thing to do was just to become parents. But we were both honest with each other in that moment, and there were a couple things that need to be shared, even though it's hard to admit.

Jonathan would have been able to drop out of school and work two jobs the next day so we would start our life that way. However, he remembered his father rarely being home, and he never wanted to be that kind of dad.

I could have also dropped out of school and become a stay-at-home mom, with Jonathan working like that. However, I knew I would regret not finishing school, and end up resenting that I had to do that.

We had only been dating four months, and though we had no intention of leaving one another, it was scary to throw our relationship into something as life-committing as parenthood.

The worst thing we had to admit to ourselves that night was that we were not the best choice for our soon-to-be child, and we wanted better for them. And trust me, it still hurts to know we were right. However, before you can see light, you have to surround yourself in darkness.

The decision was made: we were going to place our child for adoption.

Part of nourishing relationships is to understand where another's story began. Learning about Tess's story and how she methodically came to the decision she did, was a big step for myself in being able to create an authentic human connection with her. It's important to respect that everyone has a story and we can nourish the connection through understanding that. Allowing space for their story to mesh with your story, facilitates the building of a human connection.

Natural

"If the standard route for creating a family had worked for me, I wouldn't have met this child. I needed to know her. I needed to be her mother. She is, in every way, my daughter." – Nia Vardalos

Have you ever been in a situation where you are in a large group of peers and feel completely lost? It happens often in our society. You can be surrounded by people and still feel utterly alone. Why is that? Usually, it is because 1) you are sitting back and observing others creating connections without being involved, 2) you are trying too hard to make those connections and not allowing them to flow naturally, or 3) you may just not care to be connected—but I don't believe the majority of us want to feel disconnected from others. We want human connections. We *need* human connections. We thrive on making these connections. However, they don't last if they aren't formed naturally.

Now, families are created in many different ways. If all families were created the same, many of us would miss out on the opportunity to extend the arms of God to others and be blessed with their love in return. We wouldn't have the opportunity to learn and grow from the experiences with our found families that we create along our journey through life.

Also, adoption is anything but natural. It's not natural for a child to be born in this world and then to be raised by perfect strangers. So why am I talking about natural relationships being an important component of the human connection, even with adoption stories? Because all human connections need to be nurtured with a natural component. You can't force a connection to be made while also having it be authentic. It grows organically with fluid movement.

As with any relationship, if you have nourished it with time, optimism, perspective, patience, and empathy, embracing the whole relationship, a human connection with your new child will naturally progress. And just because connection with others is natural doesn't mean we sit idly by and wait for it to happen. We must play an active role in the process. Imagine transplanting a flower. It's grown in a small container at the greenhouse and then shipped to your local garden store. When you take it home, the only way for it to survive is for you to nurture it properly and then allow nature to take over. It's unnatural to be grown separate from its original home, however, it can and will thrive, naturally, when given the proper attention and nurturing.

Now, this example is specific to adoption, however the same idea rings true when forming human connections with everyone around you.

Eight years, hundreds of adoption papers, and six failed infant adoptions since our second child joined our family went by. Carl and I were so grateful for the two children we were blessed with. However, we thought we were done. Our energies were spent, our emotions were burned out, and let's face it, we were getting older. Starting over with a baby, although we would have happily done it if it happened, was not a priority anymore. It was time to give 100% of ourselves to the children we had and the open adoption relationships that we continue to build on. It's a lot to attend to seven active sets of grandparents and all the family that comes with.

One of the beautiful things of open adoption is your family grows exponentially and your reach is far beyond your own imagination. God creates families in whatever way He sees fit and we could never have orchestrated the family we now have without His grace and plan for us.

April 2017. That's when our final adoption journey began. Another great weekend away from home was being spent with Kya's birth family. Grandpa and auntie Chelsee were talking about their upcoming humanitarian trip to Ecuador. As a wanderlust myself, I was intrigued with their adventures to come and wished I could join them. Instead, I made my usual request when anyone was planning a trip to a developing country and working with orphans: "Bring me a baby home." Yes, we were done, but to be honest, I am never "done" trying to grow my family; whichever way that looks: Mother to my own children, mentor and friend for other mothers, a listening ear, a surrogate mother to orphans in developing countries, and eventually becoming a grandma myself.

Grandpa looked at me quizzically, but didn't say anything. Not ten minutes later, he asked if I was serious. I am always serious when it comes to the request of finding another child. I don't joke about being a mother to as many children as God will bless me with.

"Yes, I am serious. If you find a baby, think of us and bring them home." (As if this was the way it really worked, it's not)

"How am I supposed to choose a baby for you?"

"You chose us!"

Grandpa G was the one who found our profile online ten years earlier for Kya, our oldest. I trusted his judgment and the father figure he had become for Carl and me. And this is exactly what I told him: "I trust your judgment. If you find a baby and you feel good about it, let us know." Another curious look and that was the end of the conversation.

Four days into their service trip, Grandpa called. "I have met a little girl and I just have the strongest feeling that she needs to be in our family. You interested?" Heck yes we were, tell us more. She was 10 years old, living in an orphanage as one of the older children. She had taken on a bit of a big sister, motherly role for the other kids. Just hearing this melted my heart and I wanted to know even more. With his heart in it, having fallen in love with what could be another grandchild, Grandpa was on a mission to get her story. The very next day we found out that we were not allowed to have our choice of certain children from an international orphanage. We quickly learned that the process for an international orphan adoption is much different than a domestic infant adoption. Even more paperwork and more background checks are required, it takes more time, and there are more setbacks. Even then, you are not guaranteed a child. Once approved in the United States, you must then be approved by your country of choice, at which point you are matched with children until you decide on one or more. Phew, this was becoming a lot more than we anticipated! But then it happened—a "lightning strike moment." It is when your heart stops and you know your life is about to change drastically. It's when something literally knocks you off your feet and you just know it's the right thing to do.

A week after the first call from Grandpa, he called again, after we thought this little girl was just another dream. He said, "I am sitting in a church meeting, and someone pointed out a lady who apparently is the Director of the Board of Adoptions for Ecuador. It's not her normal church, and not a typical meeting for her to be at, but she is here." We will call her Maria. With labored breathing, our hearts pounding, we pressed him for more information. Maria told Grandpa, "Since we invited you in to volunteer in this orphanage, we can probably allow your family to choose this girl." Gasp, lightning struck!

Two years, four hundred+ pieces of paperwork, innumerable tears, thousands of heartbeats skipped, and approximately 4650 days since her arrival at the orphanage later, Yajaira joined our forever family. Clearly I have summarized this process. It was far from simple and quick. We hit every road block possible in an adoption and then some. But the point is, she is here, with us, in our family. Her story to be told for another day.

This journey was far more complicated than our other two children's adoptions. Each child comes with their own stories, and each journey was difficult in its own way, but this one taught us more life lessons than we thought possible. Now she is here. It was almost surreal to see it come into fruition. Through this adoption journey I definitely learned about how much God really does play a part in our lives. Our daughter had said many prayers while growing up in the orphanage that someday she would have a family. God heard her prayers, He heard our prayers and He answered them.

With all our adoption stories, openness and connection with the birth families has been important to us to help our children feel connected to their roots and to help their overall wellbeing. So how does open adoption play into an international orphan adoption?

We are still learning to explore this. The dialogue and conversations with Yajaira (our daughter) about her first family is very much there. She maintains regular contact with the caregivers who raised her and the other children from her "orphanage family." The day we walked away from the orphanage was just as heart wrenching as the day we walked away from the hospitals with our other two children. However, none of those moments felt like the end. We know that as we nourish these relationships, and allow them to grow naturally, they will strengthen and evolve every day. I can't wait to see where the rest of this story takes us. We strive to keep our connections as natural as possible. Letting them grow, giving them the care and attention needed to grow naturally. With this natural growth, it takes time, it doesn't happen overnight.

How natural are human connections? By our nature we are social beings. We need to connect with others to be healthy. We want our connections with others to be natural, living things, that grow and strengthen as we put time and effort into them. In *The Body is Not an Apology*, by Sonya Renee Taylor, she shares a portion of a speech given by famed author and spiritual teacher Maryanne Williamson where she discussed the principle of natural intelligence this way, "an acorn does not have to say 'I intend to become an oak tree.'" She goes on to say that natural intelligence intends that every living thing become the highest form of itself and designs us accordingly.

This is the ultimate result of all living things, its destiny: to become what it is meant to be So, if it is natural, do we necessarily need to do anything to encourage the connection?

Yes. Plants can grow without outside effort, but they can flourish with time and nurturing care. Like plants, human connections and relationships can naturally form, but they benefit more from effort. And they naturally form in their strongest forms as we exercise qualities such as optimism, patience, and empathy, as we have been discussing throughout this book.

Carl and I had been serving on the activities committee for a youth pioneer trek and would be trekking up in the mountains for a week. We had just returned home from meeting his parents to take our other two children for the week when we got another call from Grandpa. We sat on the couch looking at each other in unbelief. Had we just emotionally committed ourselves to another attempt at adoption? Were we really going to pursue providing a home and family for this beautiful young girl? She had silky smooth dark colored skin with dark black hair. She wore glasses and had crooked teeth in her smile and she smiled the biggest, most welcoming smile.

Grandpa told her about us and asked her if she wanted to be adopted. What does a ten- year-old girl say to this question? Sure? It would be nice? Responding as if it were a question for him, he told her how he would get to be her grandpa if we adopted her and how she would come to the States to live with us. He told her about Kya and Zander, and how she would be their sister. She smiled at the idea of him being her grandpa and ran into his arms with a warm and sincere embrace. I'm sure the idea of having parents and siblings encouraged such a heartfelt hug, but where she knew Grandpa already, the excitement was overwhelming. It was still a long shot for us to be able to adopt her, but just like with the other two, we had a very distinct and powerful feeling that we needed to pursue this adoption opportunity.

It didn't take me very long to get the paperwork started. Contacting a social worker who would be willing to do an international adoption home study was step one. Grandpa had found out the name of an agency in Florida that was accredited to facilitate an adoption in Ecuador from the director of adoptions in Ecuador. So I reached out to them to get the ball rolling. We also needed to connect with an agency in our home state of Idaho to orchestrate and conduct the home study. Many agencies and people are involved in the making of an adoptive family. It takes a village to bring a child to a home, just as it takes a village to raise those children.

We were both hopeful and skeptical. It's interesting how your mind can hold onto multiple emotions at the same time. It can be confusing and exhilarating. When we started the international adoption process, we were told it could take eight to twelve months, so I was sure that we would get to pick up our new daughter in April of 2018. Unfortunately, adoption is unpredictable, and I should have known better than to put my heart out there like that. To have such concrete expectations of this time frame. But I was still hopelessly optimistic.

In August of 2017, I got a call from Maria, the director of adoptions in Ecuador. She was so sweet to stay in contact with me, regardless of the restrictions of having any contact with anyone in your country of choice when adopting. She called to inform me that she would no longer be working with adoptions because her contract would likely not be renewed. I didn't exactly know what this meant, but since we had been in contact several times and she was a Godsend for my sanity, I was heartbroken to hear I wouldn't have contact with anyone on the other side. She suggested the name of someone else, but since they hadn't been a part of the process, I was hesitant to contact them for fear of our profile being compromised with the officials in Ecuador.

This call was the first of many disappointments in our journey. Lost paperwork, paperwork caught in a rainstorm that required a day or two of drying out on a table somewhere in Florida, a home study sent without a signature (this delayed the journey by four months), an accreditation that needed to be renewed unexpectedly, laws changing that required more adoption education for us. These are just a few of the delays we experienced. But God played a huge part in the journey and the timing and He knew where our journey was headed and how best to get there.

January 2018 came along. I was feeling especially anxious about this little girl and what she was doing. What were her day-to-day activities? I knew the orphanage wouldn't tell her about our journey to bring her home until we would be literally flying to her home country to pick her up. It made complete sense. No need to get her hopes up, especially since we hadn't even been officially matched with her. We knew this journey was the right thing to do, but we didn't know if it was for her or another child. We had our hearts set on her, but I would have taken all the children if they allowed it. We just knew that we would love to bring her home and welcome her to our family.

I felt a strong impression one day to reach out to Maria and let her know we were still working on our paperwork, hopeful to adopt this little girl. We had developed a bit of a relationship during our short time communicating via WhatsApp and I knew that it would be ok to contact her since her contract wasn't renewed and she no longer would be facilitating adoptions.

The thought was pretty powerful, but I brushed it aside. If God wanted it, it would happen. No need to push it, right? Wrong. I don't believe God expects us to sit back and wait. He requires us to play our part. I am not the kind of women to sit back and let things happen, anyway. I am just persistent enough to push my way through any wall that stand in my way. Miracles happen, with faith and hard work. Just as with the natural growth of a plant, you must still be actively nourishing it for it grow properly.

It took me a week to actually reach out to Maria. I knew I wanted to, but inertia is a real thing. However, when I realized that the thought was inspired from above, and that it continued to occupy my mind, it was time to just do it.

Hello Maria, it's Paula. I am so sad to not be able to work with you on this adoption; however, I did want to reach out and let you know that we are still working on our paperwork.

This is what the text read. Innocent, but informative. I wanted her to know that we were working hard on our end and that I appreciated all she did for us. Not three hours later my phone rang, with Maria on the other end.

"What is the name of the girl you want to adopt?" she asked, "Yajaira Cuchan," I replied. I heard the clicks of computer keys bouncing away on the line.

"Are you working with the ministry of adoptions still?" I asked, my curiosity building in the pit of my stomach.

"Yes, they renewed my contract. I am just looking her up in the system to see what her status is."

I waited with a lump in the back of my throat while she typed away. A short minute or two later, that felt like an hour, she informed me that Yajaira was indeed available for adoption now and that we should hurry and complete our dossier. I was so excited that it didn't dawn on me until much later that Yajaira wasn't actually available for adoption when we first heard about her from Grandpa.

Yajaira's story is quite complicated, and not one I can share at this time. However, I can say that she had been living in the orphanage for over eight years when we found her, but her mother was still around. In January 2018, during the very same week I felt so impressed to contact Maria, Yajaira's mother was finally contacted and she agreed to relinquish her rights as her mother and allow her to be adopted. This was definitely an act of God's orchestration for our family.

I got back to work on our papers just as Maria had suggested. We were only months away from April, my own perceived paper due date. That would have been ten months since hearing about Yajaira, within the eight to twelve month timeline we were led to believe was standard for such adoptions. I needed to get so many things done. The months went on, time slowly crawled by, and April came and went. Still, we were nowhere near completion of our journey. I mentioned earlier that we had more adoption credits to pass for our education requirements. With domestic infant adoptions, we had minimal amounts of adoption education requirements to meet. And we had originally submitted eleven credits, over the ten initially required. Until we were told we needed ten more credits as the requirements and laws had been adjusted by the Hague Convention, an organization that facilitates international adoption laws throughout the world.

It was as if I had just enrolled myself in a year's worth of college credits, and I was bound and determined to complete the courses within a week. I sat at our kitchen table with my computer and got to work, reading the lessons aloud for Carl to hear and participate in the courses. There was so much information. I think my chair has a permanent butt indentation from my week sitting there, only getting up for restroom breaks. My sweet husband and children helped with meals and chores so I could focus on my goal to finish in a week. That was one heck of a week, and one I will never forget as part of the daunting process we experienced in this adoption. Filling my brain with so many things and passing all the tests, spending dinners hiding behind my computer at the kitchen table while we ate, and putting in many late nights in that same chair—all worth it. In the end, I was grateful for the knowledge we gained from those courses, it was just a very daunting task. But, as in all things through this process, God set things up for our good. And for that I am thankful. We may not see it at the time, but our experiences, whether hard or easy, are for our benefit and growth. As I discuss these experiences, remember I am focusing on the natural process that takes place in human connections. Particularly in our adoption journey, the process naturally flows from one task to the next, allowing for the proper procedures to take place. Within human connections, the natural process takes place as you allow for it. Being honest and your authentic self, shine through is how this can be accomplished.

April came and went, and we were nowhere near bringing Yajaira home. We hadn't even been matched with her yet. Our dossier was still in the queue and progress was slow. Each day seemed like an eternity. Each road bump we hit, and we hit them all, made us feel like we were trying to knock down a door that wasn't meant to open. As the time dragged on, my anxiety levels built and my faith definitely wavered. Were we trying too hard to make this happen? Then I would remember how we felt when we started this journey. That "lightning strike" feeling is what kept us pushing forward. We had confirmation in our hearts that we were supposed to do this, that this connection was supposed to be.

By December of 2018, our hopes and wishes came true. Yajaira was matched with us. As Maria once told us, "the stars will need to align to have her paperwork and your dossier land on the desk of the ministry at the same time." In my heart of hearts, I see Maria as our star who helped everything align. She was placed in our path for a reason. God knew we needed her to facilitate this adoption. It was literally an answer to our prayers to be matched with Yajaira.

"You're going to be a brother/sister again," we told our two other children. The gravity of how hard it was to be matched with Yajaira hadn't quite sunk in to them, so they weren't surprised by our news. "I thought she was already coming to our home," they said. Wouldn't it be nice to have such immense faith? The thought that Yajaira would join our family was concrete for them all along. Conversely, my faith wavered often in the two long years of waiting for her. My heart was open to any child from anywhere in the world, but we had prayed for her by name each day during our adoption journey with her, and were so happy to have our prayers answered, even if it wasn't by our timetable.

We spent the next few months preparing for our new daughter to join our family, hoping and continuing to pray that nothing else would get in the way. We continued to hit road bumps, but being matched meant we were that much closer to bringing her home. At this time she was told about us and knew she was matched with a family, but we were told we still couldn't contact her. Her birthday was shortly before Christmas, but we still weren't able to connect. Due to laws, and for her safety and well-being, we were told to wait before reaching out. So we anxiously waited, and waited some more. The hardest part was the waiting when we knew she would join our family but we couldn't do anything to start building a connection with her. Night after night I would lie in bed wondering if she was okay, if they were taking care of her, if she was happy and healthy. I wanted to be able to tuck her in at night, I wanted to comfort her when she needed the love of a mother, and I just wanted to be able to hold her in my arms. I agonized over how close we were, and yet we still had no idea when we would be allowed to go get her. Remember our plant and the natural process it goes through to thrive and grow, it's a long arduous process sometimes. Plants don't sprout overnight, neither did this adoption, nor do genuine human connections. But the beauty that can be found in the wait, can be as powerful as the flower (plant) in the end.

I didn't see it at the time, since I was so anxious to get the paperwork and process moving along, but there's a natural progression that had to happen. Upon learning of Yajaira, she wasn't available for adoption at the time. The process had to move along before we could even be considered to adopt her. Her mother needed that time to relinquish her rights as her mother, regardless of that fact that Yajaira had been living in the orphanage for 8 years. Just as with human connections, time is on our side for them to grow naturally. It has been 15+ years since our first daughter was born and our relationships with all of our children's first families has taken time to grow. The time is what is natural about the process. Time is inevitable, it's going to come and go on it's own course, you can't stop it. So welcoming that and not fighting it by wishing for "quicker results" is how you naturally allow connections to happen.

April 2019. We were told to get our tickets and prepare to go. It was April, just a year later than I anticipated. Sitting at the kitchen table, my feet crossed at the ankles, I was a ball of excitement ready to explode. The pit in my stomach ached and I couldn't believe we were finally here. But fear also sat in my throat, heavy and painful. I wanted to swallow, but couldn't. What if something happened that would keep us from being able to bring her home? Regardless of that fear, I got to work making travel arrangements for Carl and me and started to plan for what our other two children would do while we were away. My in-laws graciously offered to come stay with them.

A few days later, we sat in the airport, on our way to meet with the ministry in Ecuador. It was protocol to interview with them first, so they could also evaluate us and how prepared we were to adopt an orphan, a pre-teen girl from a foreign country, with a story of her own stowed away in her proverbial baggage. The ministry wanted to ensure we were prepared for anything as it would be foolish to assume that she wasn't going to have some "baggage" from her past. While I couldn't be prepared for everything, what I could do was be prepared to love this little girl as our own, unconditionally, and bring her home into our hearts and family.

Our interview with the ministry the Friday before our introduction to our daughter was pleasant. The comfort I felt was as warm as the air outside, almost tangible, like the heavy, humid air. I was pleased with how much Spanish I understood in the meeting, really only needing the translator to confirm what I was catching in the conversation. Months of Pimsleur language studies were paying off for me now. The psychologist and director of the orphanage were there and seemed particularly interested in our well-being and state of stability. They had a close relationship with Yajaira and wanted only the best for her. I appreciated their concern, as unnerving as it was, because I knew they had Yajaira's best interest in mind.

We had already checked in to our hotel, which was more like a hostel. Her age was showing on her and the creaky tiles revealed our presence with each step. Our bed barely fit Carl's stature, but it was just what we needed. Traveling and then the interview had taken a toll on our souls. The bed was a welcomed retreat. The best part of our room was the view.

Our little hotel, which was appropriately named Perro Vago, the "Lazy Dog" in English, sat directly across the street from Yajaira's orphanage. We were on the second story of our new home for the first week in Ecuador and the concrete wall that surrounded her temporary home wasn't too tall for us to get a peek into where she was. We could see into the yard of the orphanage and hear the children playing. Little screams of joy blasted into the night air and carried into our room. This was the best part of our long weekend before getting to meet her. When not down eating at the local pizzeria for each of our meals, you could find us perched in the window, watching the children playing, hoping to catch a glimpse of her. One night Carl sat in a chair, right up next to the large window, staring out across the street. He looked like a little kid waiting up to see Santa sneak in on Christmas Eve. He was listening intently, not that we would know which playful squeals were hers, but maybe to catch a glimpse of the life she knew for the previous ten years. The children she knew as her family for so many years. We hoped to catch a peek at the circumstances in which she was living. The torture of knowing she was over there waiting for us to come get her was almost too much for me to bear. Was she happy? Was she as nervous as we were? She knew we were coming. I hoped that she was as excited as we were. I watched Carl watch, and meandered over to the window to look for myself occasionally. My stomach was both a hollow pit and full of butterflies. We were so close, and still had to wait.

It was a long weekend for us, meeting with the ministry and being scrutinized in person, as opposed to solely being judged on our paper life, which they had laid out in front of them. It was long because we waited in the warm South American air to meet our little girl. It was long because we watched from so close as she went about her days without us. Monday had to come sometime, but it wasn't fast enough. Finally, it did come. My nerves were on fire. I was so excited to see our new daughter.

Meeting her for the first time was a dream come true. As I mentioned before, the orphanage itself was surrounded by a concrete wall and an iron gate for entrance. You only could enter after ringing a loud bell that echoed through the neighborhood. We rang that bell and were admitted with the psychologist and case worker. We sat in a little room the size of a large laundry room; in fact, I believe there was a small sink adjacent to two worn down love seats. The only light in the room crept in from the windows covered with bars. I don't know if it was more for the protection or an aesthetic choice for the area.

As we sat in the small darkened room, we waited with much anticipation to meet her. We had gifts and balloons for her as a celebratory gesture—something more than our emotions to mark the moment. At times I felt like they were dragging the wait out, just so the moment we met her would be that much more exciting. I didn't particularly need that anticipation; I was already excited. Carl squeezed my hand in his own anticipation. Then they opened the door, and there she was, peeking slowly around the psychologist who allowed her in. Then she ran into my arms. She ran and didn't let go. Carl wrapped his arms around the both of us like he didn't want to let go. After several moments, with tears rolling down my face, she released her grip around my waist, just long enough to transfer her arms around Carl's mid-section. It was then my turn to wrap my arms around them. The intense embrace she gave us assured me that she was in this for the long haul. Deep down, I was preparing myself for whatever challenges would come with adopting a tween orphan, but I knew it was all going to be all right the moment I saw her run to us.

We knew we had a long way to go to make the necessary connection with this child. She would be coming to us with history, with potential psychological and emotional issues. It was a given. But the moment we embraced her was the moment I knew our emotional connection had begun. It felt natural to hold her in that moment. It was the natural progression from the journey we had been on and a natural reaction for her, who had been waiting so long for a family to care for her. She was ready to give herself to our family and to the many human connections she would make in her future. A very different future than I think even she imagined just weeks before. Authenticity and vulnerability play a huge role in a genuine human connection. I was ready for that, and I felt she was ready. When we embrace the possibility of connection without reservation, we allow our bonds with others to form naturally, to start from a place of optimism as we commit to willingly nourish the relationship.

In the two years that she has been in our home, we have faced some challenges, naturally, nothing we weren't expecting. It could be that we were mentally prepared for them, or it could be the simple fact that she is very resilient and ready to endure the challenges ahead of her. Things like learning a new language, learning what it's like to be a part of a family, learning the cultures of a new environment, experiencing life with siblings. Although with as many children as were in the orphanage, I believe her biggest challenge with this was that there were now only two other kids to interact with, and those two kids had a very different view of life from what she grew up with.

None of this experience is natural, starting your life over completely for Yajaira, or welcoming a new sibling for Kya and Zander. Not natural processes for your typical family dynamic. But with love and care, connections can be strengthened from the qualities mentioned throughout this book. Optimism, accepting obtainability in relationships, perspective and being persistent, patience is definitely a principal component. Embracing other's differences and allowing for an all-encompassing, unconditional love to be present are important. Empathy plays a huge role in allowing for authentic connections to be nourished properly for natural growth. The true nature in a connection comes from all these qualities and accepting that it takes time and time isn't always on our side. Patience, authentic connections will come. These are what we have learned from our open adoptions and fostering genuine human connections.

Being authentically you

"I've learned that people will forget what you said, people will forget what you did, but people will never forget how you made them feel" – Maya Angelou

Growing up in the military and moving from place to place every couple of years taught me a lot about making connections quickly. I imagine our daughter, Yajaira, learned a lot of the same lessons in her early childhood. Kids would come and go from the orphanage, either back with family or leaving to be adopted, and she also moved between different orphanages.

Frequent changes, like moving to a new town, or to a new orphanage, requires a person to learn flexibility in order to adapt to a new environment. Though important, being flexible does have its challenges. It's easy to get caught up in what I like to call "chameleon conformity," where we become someone we are not to adapt to our surroundings, or the people in them. However, this does not allow for true human connection because it isn't authentic. Rather, healthy flexibility and adaptability means being authentically yourself as you allow others the same privilege. It is recognizing who you are and choosing who you want to be in your relationship with others, not conforming to other's ideas to who you are.

Offering your true self is the goal for real human connections. When you become someone you are not, what are you really giving to others in a relationship? In a podcast called "Being Seen" by JennyQ, the host uses her guests stories and her own life experiences to show listeners how "being seen" by another human being is one way for people to make authentic human connections. She points out that the willingness to be vulnerable, to allow others to "see" the true us, is equally as important as opening our eyes to others' stories and offering them a chance to be seen. Being vulnerable shows who we really are, there's nothing to hide in vulnerability. But of course being vulnerable with ourselves first, through an honest set of eyes allows for more compassion in seeing others' for who they really are, or at least allow to be seen. Its not easy to be vulnerable and show your true self in the public eye. We want to show our best selves. It's a social phenomenon that we show our best day, and then we ourselves compare our worst day to someone's best day. How is that fair and honest? It's not, which is why it's important to allow vulnerability to play an role in building authentic human connection. I'm not saying we always need to air out our dirty laundry for all to see. However, sometimes when people show themselves at their best, it can be uplifting and motivating on our messy days. But it's even more refreshing to see that other's struggle the same way we do; vulnerability.

In the first week with your child in an international adoption, at least with ours, you spend it under the careful eyes of the adoption team, including a psychologist. You really can't hide anything, as the bonding period needs to be authentic in order for a successful adoption to occur. If we wanted this little girl to be able to get to know her new parents and understand what her new life would be, we had to adapt to our environment with our real selves. Putting on a façade could be damaging to her future because it wouldn't be authentic.

As we got to know Yajaira and saw who she was, and how she interacted with us, the case worker, the psychologist, and the other children, it was evident that she had nothing to hide. Her life was as transparent as a window. She offered us the gift of her authentic self as we started to form the all-important personal human connections that help bring us together as family, instead of strangers.

This need for authenticity holds true in all lasting connections, adoptive or not. Hiding away from who you really are is as damaging to a connection as fire is to a beautifully crafted painting. Our masterpieces, created as we follow God's plan for us in faith, make up who we are. When we are true to ourselves, we are more open to composing a beautiful tapestry of healthy, authentic, and long-lasting relationships with others.

As you come to understand and share your authentic self with others, it is important to be aware of the fragility of human emotions. We have recently been connected to some of Yajaira's biological siblings. We are carefully and delicately moving forward in forming a relationship with them.

With our other two children, we were able to form open and authentic relationships with their birth families from the very beginning. We've had years and years to build our family relationships, even before the birth of each of our children. An open adoption has been their reality and their normal from the beginning, and the human connections between our families grew naturally as we invested time, love, and understanding into our relationships with each other.

Now, we have a young impressionable daughter with the sting of her very different, previous life still fresh on her mind. Because she is an older adoptee, we haven't had the years of connection with her family to rely on as we navigate her new life together. There is an important connection there to be had, but if we want it to be a healthy, happy, authentic human connection, we must give careful attention to everyone involved. As we nurture any relationship, like the care of a delicate flower, love must abound. This is why I so intently focus on the qualities described in this book as key ideas to consider in creating authentic human connections..

Do you remember the story of when we blessed our six-month-old son on our oldest daughter's third birthday? We had so many family members there—my family and Carl's, our daughter's birth mom and dad and their families, and our son's birth mom and dad and their families.

This single event offered us the opportunity to grow together in ways that created a beautiful piece of artwork. Connections were being made all around our little family of four, and it was an integral moment in the development of how our open adoption story would play out in the years to come. God knew it all along and was just waiting for us to see it

Connection is an ever changing journey that needs to allow for growth, change, and understanding. Respect the process. True connections take time. As mentioned earlier, it has taken years for us to build the close connections we have in our open adoptions.

Sure, we created superficial connections in the beginning. Simple conversations, initial eye contact, and other minor, surface-level actions are what get connections started. They form the baseline, the initial blueprints of the connection you hope to build. But the deep authentic human connections occur when we nurture the connections and allow time for the growth to happen.

Now, the process of building deep connections is often messy. We are human after all, and humanity is imperfect by nature. No matter how similar or close you are to a person, conflict is inevitable. It's a natural part of the process as you find where you fit, learn where you are different, and adjust to each other. But through this messy process comes authenticity. And open communication, charitable love, respect, and empathy for the other's point of view will help you resolve conflicts as they arise.

The journey of authentic human connections requires us to take action. Like love, connection is an action verb. It is something we must put time and effort into if we want it to succeed. It is something we must do and put in the time for it all to be worth it.

Let's revisit the acronym "Open" to highlight the key things we've learned about creating healthy, lasting, deep human connections and relationships. Since the God-given blessing of my family's open adoptions have taught me so much about the importance of openness in human connections.

O-Obtainability and **Optimism**. Letting God be your composer and having faith in His plan for you will help direct you to the authentic relationships you desire. And opening your heart to the qualities we've discussed in this book will allow you to accept and embrace the relationships you would like to have.

I am a believer in karma--what we put out into the universe will ultimately come back to us a hundredfold. So, when building relationships with others, I want to be as optimistic as I can. I want to put forth the effort to be positive and optimistic, to look for the good. I want to turn the connections I form with others around me into opportunities for myself and others to "be seen" as JennyQ teaches.

P-Perseverance and **Perspective**. Obtaining or building human connections doesn't happen overnight and it doesn't happen without conscious effort on our part. In my faith, there is a saying about God: "He never said it would be easy; He only said it would be worth it." Pushing through the messy and the hard is what builds our character into who we want to be. If a connection is important to you, you will see it through the tough times and the conflicts. If you are willing to grow together and to have empathy for each other, then your connection can grow and strengthen as you persevere together.

With perseverance comes patience. I used to think that being patient was as simple as waiting for something that ultimately would happen. But true patience involves having compassion for yourself and others, and keeping a positive outlook on the end result. Waiting for something can be frustrating, but true patience comes when you work to let go of the frustration and enjoy the journey. Forming lasting connections takes time and requires patience for both your own imperfections and the imperfections of others. Life is never perfect, and sometimes is far from what we initially imagined, but with real patience, the beauty of the experience shines through and strong connections can be forged.

How we look at our experiences in our human connections is vital to our own growth., so our perspective of our connections must be handled with particular care. I've said it before and I'll say it again: human connection is a beautifully messy journey. Having your eyes open to all possibilities with an optimistic and empathetic view keeps your connections real because you are willing to have compassion for yourself and the other person while looking for ways to deeply connect.

E-Embrace and **Empathy.** I can't talk enough about the importance of these words. Everyone has a story they bring to the table and everyone's story is unique. Being able to own who you are and bring that story to a relationship is where authenticity lies. When you finally embrace your true self, you can honestly and wholeheartedly contribute to a connection. As Brene Brown puts it, owning your story is the bravest thing you can do.

If owning your story is the bravest thing you can do, then I say that accepting another's story is the most charitable and empathetic thing you can do. Empathy is loving and embracing others. It is walking in another's shoes, even for a moment, to better understand them. Empathy is seeing others for who they are, recognizing what they can contribute, and seeing them with unconditional love.

To truly exhibit an all-encompassing love for others, you need to have a forgiving and graceful heart. Encompassing love forgives imperfections and allows grace for mistakes and conflicts as you work to build connections. Encompassing love means you go into new situations with eyes wide open, knowing there will be difficulties, accepting the messiness as you find the good and work through the hard parts.

N-Nourish and **Natural**. When I was a little girl, I had a pet gecko. Unfortunately, I forgot about it and forgot to feed it, until one day I went to check on him and he was dead. Regretfully, I most certainly did not nourish him well. Like all living things, true connections with others require nourishment to survive. If you don't devote time, energy, and attention to your relationships, they will eventually fizzle out and die. True connections grow and stretch as you both accept each other as you are now, and work together to grow into the best version of yourselves that you can be.

Remember that it's natural for relationships and the human connection to go through ebbs and flows or good and bad. Be patient, and accept that connections won't always look the way you may have dreamt they would. There is a natural progression of growth over time and with hard work. But don't forget to enjoy the journey!

We are given choices to make every day of our lives. We can choose to have patience with others. We can choose to be persistent in our kindness for others. We can choose to be optimistic and to look for the good and for what we can learn in our interactions with others. In fact, the perspective we approach relationships with is often directly relevant to the ultimate result. Authentic human connections can be obtained when we embrace who we really are and embrace the truth behind another's façade. Love, an all-encompassing love, an unconditional love, must be present for authenticity in the human connection. Let your relationships flow naturally and nourish them often.

Like the beloved cartoon character Ms. Frizzle, from *The Magic School Bus,* likes to say, "Take chances, make mistakes, get messy." Without the connections I've been blessed with, my canvas was too clean and white, . You may even say it was boring from an artist's perspective. Each connection I've made has brought color, depth, and added meaning to the canvas. The composition is personal, stained with a rainbow of connections. Each brush stroke is an experience, each drop of color is a human connection, and each piece is as unique as the people that color it. When I take a moment to view my personal canvas, I can see that it's beautiful, all the imperfections and stories brought together into a cohesive, connected whole. As we "open" ourselves to authentic human connections, our lives become richer and happier. May we all see the marvelous work that God has created for each of us as we stumble toward becoming His masterpieces through authentically connecting with others around us.